D0969350

BECOME AN INNER CIRCLE ASSISTANT

How to be a Star in Your Profession and
Achieve Inner Circle Status

By Joan M. Burge

INSIGHT PUBLISHING
SEVIERVILLE, TENNESSEE

Become an Inner Circle Assistant

© Copyright Joan M. Burge, 2005

All rights reserved. No part of this book may be reproduced in any form or by any means without prior written permission from the publisher except for brief quotations embodied in critical essay, article, or review. These articles and/or reviews must state the correct title and contributing author of this book by name.

Published by Insight Publishing Company
P.O. Box 4189
Sevierville, Tennessee 37864

10 9 8 7 6 5 4 3 2

Printed in The United States

ISBN: 1-932863-50-8

TABLE OF CONTENTS

ACKNOWLEDGEMENTS

Little did I know this book would be a 35-year work in progress. That's not how long it took me to write it, of course, but that is how long I have worked with the administrative profession. In fact, for the last 15 of those years, I have dedicated myself to teaching others in the field how to advance their careers, improve the quality of their work lives and gain greater satisfaction from their chosen career. In other words, I have shown them how to be stars in the administrative world.

The stories in this book are those of real people who have also worked in the field. It is only natural, then, that I acknowledge and thank the thousands of assistants, executive assistants, office administrators, administrative coordinators and others in this business who have touched my life since 1970. I have had a wonderful journey working with so many talented people. I am also thankful for all the great bosses I had during my career as an assistant, who made me feel like I was part of their team and taught me that my value was equal to that of their senior executives.

I especially appreciate my wonderful clients who have entrusted their administrative staff to me in their quest for excellence. I have learned as much from them as they have from me.

I want to express my profound appreciation to my wonderful husband, Dave, who has always supported me in my career endeavors and has been my cheerleader and business coach. I am also thankful to all my family and friends, especially my daughter, Lauren, and my son, Brian. They have generously shared me with the world. Special thanks also go out to my sister, Gina, who freely shares her creative ideas with me, and my father, Anthony DeGirolamo, who has always been a great entrepreneur and inspiration to me! And I would be remiss if I didn't mention our two golden retrievers, Annie and Zoe.

There are many others who have helped give birth to this book since April 2004, including Mike McCallister, president & CEO, Humana Inc. He was kind enough to write the Foreword and has been very supportive of my work since 1998. He is also a firm believer in the profession and the value assistants bring to an organization. Thanks also to Marilyn Pincus, Rita Rozencrantz, Russ Hollingsworth and his staff at Insight Publishing, and Mitch Moore. And a special note of appreciation goes to my own *inner circle* assistant, Dawn Lesser, who has kept the office running smoothly while I've been working on this book!

Finally, I must express how thankful I am for each and every person who has crossed my path during my two careers; I have learned from all of you!

DEDICATION

This book is dedicated to my husband, Dave, and my two new grandsons, Jeffrey Bradley and Eian Christopher. May they always follow their dreams and go after life with great hope, energy and enthusiasm.

FOREWORD

For more than a decade, Joan Burge has led the way in articulating and implementing a new vision for one of the most vital and overlooked professions in American business—the executive assistant. As chief executive officer of a large health benefits company, I can testify to the importance of the executive assistant role and to the value Joan has brought not only to the profession as a whole but to the many Humana executive assistants who have grown, changed and successfully assumed expanded responsibilities through her Star Achievement Series® program over the past few years.

In *Become an Inner Circle Assistant*, Joan outlines what it takes to become a value-added partner—for your supervisor and for the enterprise as a whole. This is ultimately what any good boss wants from his or her executive assistant: someone who suggests the best sense of the now-discredited word "secretary." The original meaning of secretary was not "someone who answers the phone and types 80 words a minute." It was "someone who could keep secrets"—a person so alert, well-trained, well-spoken and attuned to a manager's needs, that he or she could be trusted with strategic information that was crucial to success. It is this sense of trustworthiness, born of key skills and the right personal qualities, that lies at the heart of Joan's concept of becoming an *inner circle* assistant.

As with her Star Achievement Series® curriculum, this book is loaded with practical, step-by-step guidance on how to achieve the standards she sets for the next-generation executive assistant. There is a detailed road map to success, including descriptions of 12 competency areas designed to make the executive assistant a key player on the management team. There is an appropriate emphasis on the basics, because some things never change. There is a robust description of the advantages to the assistant and to the enterprise of membership in the *inner circle*. And—typical of Joan—there is emphasis on the sheer fun you derive from your work when you've earned and are recognized for your *inner circle* status.

I don't know of anyone better than Joan Burge to guide executive assistants into the 21st century. With her trademark combination of hard-minded, research-based advice and her unparalleled respect for the profession's importance, she instills—with wit and enthusiasm—the courage to excel.

Michael B. McCallister
President and Chief Executive Officer
Humana Inc.[1]

---

[1] (*Humana Inc., headquartered in Louisville, Kentucky, is one of the nation's largest publicly traded health benefits companies, with approximately 5.8 million medical members located primarily in 15 states and Puerto Rico. Humana Inc. is a Fortune 200 company with revenues of approximately $12.2 billion*)

DEAR READER

At the writing of this book, more women than men hold administrative assistant positions in the United States. That may change because the *inner circle* assistant in no way resembles the secretary of yesteryear. That individual sat at a desk and typed, answered telephones, followed orders and took home a modest paycheck. A career secretary generally attached herself to a successful boss, and that boss was, with rare exception, a man. It's not surprising that the work was considered "woman's work." New times call for new measures, and the Stars and World Class administrative professionals of today play a different role in the company. Their work is exciting, challenging and fulfilling, and salaries reflect how companies assess their value. In addition to typing and handling telephones, these employees take initiative, get involved, think and act like partners. Not only do they operate software programs, they meet with vendors to discuss modifications, pricing and needs. Their contributions impact the company's bottom line. An article entitled "What Americans Earn" in a June 1995 *Fortune* magazine article reported that the typical top pay of the executive secretary was $70,000. And if you prefer to rely upon the U.S. Bureau of Labor statistics, you'll find that median annual earnings of executive secretaries and administrative assistants were $31,090 in 2000 and that the highest 10 percent earned more than $46,000. In many ways, this profession changed while almost no one was looking. And many people still don't realize how much things have changed. Once they do, there's every reason to believe that more women and men, too, will aspire to be Stars and World Class administrative professionals. For now, however, I've taken the liberty of writing my book relying heavily upon the pronouns "she" and "her." I offer this explanation in order to allay any concerns that I have overlooked anyone.

Joan Burge

INTRODUCTION:
A ROAD MAP AND A REFERENCE BOOK

Today's *inner circle* assistant enjoys rewards her pioneer sisters and brothers never dreamed possible.

The *inner circle* assistant is:

- *Appreciated for her ability and entrusted with more sensitive, insider information so that she's poised to contribute.*
- *Treated like a business partner. It follows that she thinks like a business partner. She doesn't wait for an invitation to get involved. She's always involved.*
- *Receiving across-the-board-support that a less involved administrative assistant would never be granted. Doors open for her because now she's an insider.*
- *Finding work to be challenging, calling upon cognitive powers. The train-for-the-task strategy isn't supreme in this venue; rather, senses are engaged and brainpower is on call. She doesn't wait for things to happen and then act or decide what to do; she makes things happen. She knows how both the executive she supports and her company will benefit.*

No matter whether you view your job as a career, a stepping-stone to another position, or strictly work that brings in a paycheck, *Become an Inner Circle Assistant* supports you as you carve out your place in the sun. It's loaded with tips, strategies and methods you can use. You'll even be introduced to new possibilities, a wish list of things you may never have thought to ask for, such as eliminating busywork. It's a snap to do once you establish a new level of communication with the executive(s) you support.

In fact, there are chapters in Section III that give you the how-to-do-it details you need to not only eliminate busywork but to make dozens of important good-for-the-company and good-for-you wishes come true.

What You Get

The book is filled with road maps for success. You'll find self-scoring quizzes, real-life stories and examples to help make the journey both pleasant and relevant to your specific needs.

Repetition is a powerful learning technique. If you ever helped a child master spelling words, you've witnessed the process in action. "See it, say it and spell it. See it, say it and spell it." After some repetition, most children know and remember how to spell the word.

In the same way, you'll return to portions of the book to renew and refresh information you missed the first time. It's a rare individual who ingests how-to-do-it information and uses it all effectively after being exposed to it only once.

Become an Inner Circle Assistant also serves as a reference book. Do you currently judge yourself to be very capable at organizing the office or solving problems? These are just two of a dozen Key Competencies you'll find discussed in detail. Review them to see how you measure up. Return to them from time to time and ask yourself, "How am I doing?" The dozen Key Competencies lay out the basics and then show you how to build on or enhance them. If we're to embrace Dr. Covey's Sharpen the Saw approach to excellence, we must ask ourselves from time to time, "How are we doing?" (Sharpening the Saw is the phrase that best describes the seventh step in Stephen R. Covey's book *The 7 Habits of Highly Effective People*. This step spotlights all aspects of self-renewal—mental, physical, emotional and spiritual.)

To the Moon

Remember Jackie Gleason's television character Ralph Kramden from *The Honeymooners*? One of Kramden's favorite sayings, usually directed to his wife, Alice, was "Bang, zoom, right to the moon!" No matter how often Gleason said "To the moon," he never made it sound used or worn out. His delivery was always enthusiastic!

Since the inception of Office Dynamics, Ltd., in 1988, I've been intensely aware of the ongoing changes in this profession. I've shared my observations with thousands of seminar attendees and workshop participants. I never tire of saying some version of *to the moon*. People who groom themselves to excel in this career have nowhere to go but up — to the top!

I've enjoyed writing *Become an Inner Circle Assistant*. My enthusiasm is every much as potent as Ralph Kramden's. You can find your way to the top of your profession, to the stars, to the moon! Nothing would please me more than to see you there.

In the words of Henry David Thoreau, "I know of no more encouraging fact than the unquestioned ability of a man to elevate his life by conscious endeavor."

Let's add the word "woman" to this quote.

This applies to you!

Inner Circle

S E C T I O N   O N E

A New Way of Looking at This Profession

What's Different Now?
What Can You Do About It?
What Does It Mean To You?

CHAPTER 1

What's Different Now?

Not too long ago, I conducted assistant/manager partnership workshops and consulted with high-level executives at a major corporation. I want to share with you a sampling of what I heard from the other side of the desk.

Two things stood out:

1. Managers have a good perspective of what they think the administrative professional's role should be and what the team relationship should look like.
2. Managers target areas of growth for their assistants—things that really frustrate them or tasks they feel their assistants should be doing and are not doing.

Managers perceive that the administrative professional of today should:

- *Use good judgment.*
- *Be an advisor.*
- *Direct "issues" to the right person.*
- *Shadow the boss; when the boss isn't in, shadow his views of situations, know how he or she might respond to a situation and then act.*
- *Be service oriented; help people, including internal customers (e.g., other employees), as well as the external customers.*

- *Be a barometer; have a sense for the issues that are taking place. And also be able to tell the boss when he/she makes a decision that maybe isn't the best decision.*
- *Keep the boss updated on what's going on in the office.*
- *Attend staff meetings.*
- *"Manage up." In other words, the administrator should push or encourage the manager when necessary.*

This same group of managers viewed the ideal assistant/manager team relationship as follows. They:
- *Engage in open and frequent communication.*
- *Exchange ideas and use one another as a sounding board.*
- *Trust one another and enjoy mutual respect.*
- *Like one another.*
- *Encourage professional development for both parties.*
- *Work together to establish efficient daily, weekly and monthly routines.*
- *Provide resources, remove barriers.*
- *Don't hesitate to give an occasional pat on the back.*
- *Are able to disagree.*
- *Are sensitive to each other's needs.*
- *Determine each team member's style and fit those styles to each part of any project.*

High-level executives value assistants who:
- *Have a positive attitude.*
- *Take the initiative to make changes when warranted.*
- *Can solve problems.*
- *Take ownership in the company (e.g., feel proud of the company and speak and act accordingly).*
- *Get engaged in what their bosses are involved in.*
- *Can make a difference.*

- *Take ownership of things in the department (e.g., assumes responsibility).*
- *Are customer service oriented.*
- *Finish a project or task, even as minor as taking a thorough telephone message.*
- *Demonstrate leadership.*
- *Share.*
- *Listen carefully so that accurate reporting is possible.*
- *Are resourceful.*

If you showed the above list to a secretary who toiled in the workplace many years ago, she would be amazed. Today, this kind of participation is expected. There's nothing unusual about what these managers think of as vital. I certainly have heard it all before.

In order to make the best use of this feedback, let's get specific. As we examine *what's new, what you can do about it* and *what it means to you*, we'll spotlight one or more of the Key Competencies (i.e., responsibilities), and we'll use illustrations to demonstrate what's new.

Later in this book, we'll discuss each of the competencies in detail. Right now, let's focus on the fact that the job has changed dramatically. You're about to discover that the managers' seemingly overwhelming list is not overwhelming to everyone. The *inner circle* assistant is already turning in an award-winning performance!

TWELVE KEY COMPETENCIES

1. Appointment Coordination
2. Manager Support
3. Managing Office Technology

Illustration

MANAGER SUPPORT: *Today's inner circle assistant does not wait to be told what to do; she's an initiator.* For example, my assistant, Dawn, sets up my trip to Miami. She arranges for the airplane tickets, hotel rooms and rental car, but she doesn't stop there. Dawn looks for additional speaking opportunities for me while I'm in Miami.

Why? She knows that in my business, the more exposure I get, the more paid speaking invitations I'll receive. She obtains the name and phone number for the person who books programs for the Miami Rotary Club and one or two other organizations. She spotlights groups with members who may have need of my services.

If you ask Dawn, "What does Joan do?" she won't say, "My boss is a speaker" and leave it at that. She understands the scope of my business and helps to run it.

If you ask me, "What does Dawn do?" I won't say, "She types and answers the telephone" and leave it at that. If I did, my response would fall far short of explaining her importance to the company.

Illustration

OFFICE ORGANIZATION: *Today's inner circle assistant works with the executive she supports to establish efficient daily, weekly and monthly routines and takes ownership of things in the department.* The reality that none of us is spared from family crises or personal medical problems should motivate us to have a fallback plan. My dad and brother-in-law, who are business partners, had no one in the wings who could pick up the work for them. Although they had been told for years, "You better train someone to do what you do," they thought the day would never come when they would both be away from work. But in fact, that's exactly what happened. Life happens and so do tragic events.

I know it's hard to make time to write a desk description guide or train colleagues on certain aspects of your job. However, if you should have to be away for any length of time from your job, the chaos created is far more troublesome than investing an hour here and there. Years ago, when my previous assistant Stacie started her job, I was adamant that she write a Desk Reference Manual. I knew this would be a big project, but the approach I recommended was that as she worked on projects, she could document that information on her computer. As she developed forms or created correspondence, she made extra copies to insert in her manual to act as samples. When she took on a new project with several steps, she documented every step. As Stacie worked on her manual in installments, she would show her progress to me. I was quite impressed. After 10 months, she had an excellent reference and how-to manual. Stacie included where to go and whom to call, my travel preferences, emergency numbers and important contacts. She not only wrote excellent content but she livened it up with graphics!

You might want to seriously consider writing a manual. A manual is especially useful for those who have to step in when you are out of the office. Stacie developed 22 sections. Here are a few of the categories she created:

- *Mission Statement*
- *Organization Chart*
- *Routines*
- *Telephones/Voice Mail*
- *Computer Files*
- *Travel*

- *Computer Equipment*
- *Repairs*
- *People You Should Know (e.g., accountant, attorney)*

In past years, an outside consultant may have been called upon to write this manual. It would not occur to the executive or to his assistant that she could rise to the occasion. Today, it's a new ballgame!

CHAPTER 2

What Can You Do About It?

Start by seeing yourself in a new light. Perception is a powerful phenomenon. Your view, your opinion or your assessment of something influences the way you act. The same is true for others. Even if you have two years to go before retirement, why shouldn't you make the most of your on-the-job hours? You're in an exciting profession but only if you see it for what it is and act accordingly. Be proactive and there's no telling where it will lead.

Make Time for Introspection!

One would hope we think about many things all day long, but do you ever take time to think about yourself?

- *Who are you?*
- *How do others see you?*
- *What do you think about the issues of the day and why?*
- *Are you easily swayed by what others say, or do you allow yourself to come to your own conclusions?*
- *What do you want to do with your life?*

If you gain a full sense of who you are, you can't help but be more confident at work and in relationships. You'll be assertive when you need to be and able to lead others rather than be led. You'll recognize opportunities and you'll seize them.

Introduce Yourself to Yourself

You're not the person you once were. Times change. People change. You have changed, too. You owe it to yourself to make time for introspection so that you're not a stranger to yourself. Don't wait for quiet time to open up because it never will. There will always be a project to work on, family demands, another errand to run, another memo to write.

Schedule time for getting to know yourself. When the time arrives, ask questions. As you search for answers, avoid knee-jerk responses, which tend to camouflage the truth. For example, if you ask yourself "Where do I want to go?" and the answer is "I want to work for this company until I retire, and I'll do my best to keep my job," it may be the answer your spouse or friends expect from you. If so, you're operating on automatic pilot! Perhaps you would really like to work for a top executive instead of a middle manager. If so, say so. Soon you may think about steps to take to groom yourself for the job. There's a very slim chance that you'll ever work for a top executive unless you know that is what you want to do.

Are You Courageous?

Don't neglect to ask yourself about courage. Courage is that inner quality you possess that enables you to face challenges (e.g., change) and act without showing fear. When you're in your introspection mode, try using the following Courage Meter.

Activity: Rate your ability to display courage by placing an X in the appropriate box.

Never	Seldom	Sometimes	Often	
☐	☐	☐	☐	I accept what I can't change.
☐	☐	☐	☐	I overcome obstacles.
☐	☐	☐	☐	I go after what I believe in.
☐	☐	☐	☐	I am willing to take risks.
☐	☐	☐	☐	I propose needed change.
☐	☐	☐	☐	I uphold personal values and morals.
☐	☐	☐	☐	I stick up for my associates.
☐	☐	☐	☐	I show self-confidence.
☐	☐	☐	☐	I initiate necessary communication.
☐	☐	☐	☐	I am a role model for co-workers and subordinates.
☐	☐	☐	☐	I am open to new ideas.
☐	☐	☐	☐	I reach beyond my known limitations.
☐	☐	☐	☐	I don't allow negatives to interfere with my attitude or work.

COURAGE METER KEY:

ALREADY IN *Inner Circle* Territory
Often = 10-13 checkmarks

NOT YET in *Inner Circle* Territory
Sometimes = 9 or more checkmarks
Often & Always = less than a total of 3

NEED WORK
Never & Seldom = the only columns checked

SCORE: If you fall into the NEEDS WORK category, there's a good chance you're not being kind or candid with yourself. If you score in the *Inner Circle* Territory, congratulations! NOT YET in *Inner Circle* Territory suggests that you're a viable candidate!

It's useful to realize that you're presented with opportunities to show courage every day. Courage *is in the mix* when you're:

- *Dealing with a colleague who is ignoring the consequences of his or her actions.*
- *Confronting someone about a negative attitude.*
- *Not giving up because an idea you offered was rejected.*
- *Being honest with a coworker even when you expect disagreement.*
- *Learning new things.*
- *Changing your attitude about events and people.*
- *Being flexible.*

If your Courage Meter score falls short of where you want it to be, select a scenario that tests your performance. Pick from these spotlighted opportunities or pick another. Now comes the fun part! Adapt the thirteen chart declarations to the scenario. For example: "When learning new things, I accept what I can't change. I overcome obstacles. I go after what I believe in. I am willing to take risks. I propose needed changes." Adapt this strategy and you'll be giving your courage the equivalent of a year's membership in the local gym. You will strengthen it!

Are You Easily Intimidated?

This is another good question to ask yourself during a period of introspection. That's because feeling intimidated is self-limiting.

- *It holds you back from being the best you can be or from offering good suggestions to improve work conditions.*
- *It can lower your sense of self-worth.*
- *It stunts professional and personal growth and doesn't allow your star qualities to shine.*

You may not realize that this heavy weight is chained to your ankles. If you look down and find it there, get ready to break the chain.

Such things as another person's title or tone of voice intimidate some people. Some feel intimidated when a coworker is opinionated and speaks loudly, stands too close or is considerably taller.

It's likely that each of us feels intimidated on occasion, but it's very helpful to combat the feeling because it's plain old not good for you!

Tips You Can Use:

- *Use positive self-talk.*
- *Tell yourself, "No one can make me feel intimidated unless I cooperate!"*
- *Speak clearly and firmly yet pleasantly with others.*
- *Reinforce confidence with gesture and posture. Stand straight. Don't slouch.*

- *Become knowledgeable on a wide range of subjects.*
- *Be sure to learn about your work, department and industry.*
- *Don't avoid people who intimidate you.*

You may eventually intimidate others with the confidence you exude! Being intimidated is bad for you, but it's also true that if you intimidate others (in a very professional manner), you may reach your objectives with greater ease. This strategy makes the most of your understanding of the human condition. During periods of introspection, you have time to consider such matters and feel buoyed by this knowledge.

After you tap into this reservoir of information about yourself, notify yourself that you're in charge: "I've got five years of valuable experience behind me, and I can build upon that." Find a way to do what you want to do. You may need others to help you reach goals. Reach out to those folks. It's impractical to wait and see if someone will come and take you by the hand. Moreover, the journey to attain your goal should fill you with excitement and bring you joy. (Did you ever hear the saying, "Getting there is half the fun"?)

When life pitches you curves, conjure up creative ways to knock them out of the ballpark. You might get knocked down, but you don't have to stay down. Pick yourself up and get on with it.

Illustration

Cheryl, a fictitious administrative assistant I've created for the purpose of this illustration, represents dozens of administrative assistants whom I've met and from whom I've learned so much.

Cheryl was given too much to do and too little time in which to do it. Some of the work was unfamiliar to her, and yet, her manager assumed she would handle it. And handle it she did. She

13

went to different colleagues for assistance. Each one was able to add a piece to her puzzle, but she never felt as though she was on solid ground when she turned in this work. She frequently worked overtime, but her manager didn't care. He left the office most days at five o'clock while she toiled at her desk.

Cheryl scheduled some time for introspection and admitted to herself that she tended to be a perfectionist. When she had to deal with these *stressors*, she couldn't possibly deliver the high quality of work she wanted to deliver. She had been living in a pressure cooker for the last three years, and she wanted to turn off the heat! She didn't want to risk losing her job, but she knew that she hated to compromise the quality of her work. She rarely finished out a workweek feeling satisfied, and no one ever said thank you for a job well done. She wanted to be appreciated!

Cheryl was exhausted. She rarely had time to do anything but chores in her private hours. She had given up planting flowers and tending the garden she loved. Her husband frequently told her to calm down. Had she grown more irritable? She knew that she wasn't sleeping well. Her forced self-introspection experience was very telling.

If Cheryl came to you for advice, you might tell her to:

- *Discuss your job description with your boss. Ask him if he wants to add the new work to your regular duties. Let him know that you need more training to do this work well. Ask him to suggest how you can obtain that training. In short, communicate! Don't suffer in silence, and don't settle for the same old stuff.*

- *Make a decision not to work overtime unless there's a true emergency. If you feel anxious because the work isn't finished, remind yourself that you'll be more productive and happier when you have sufficient time away from the office. You were hired for a 40-hour workweek and that's that.*

- *Consider delegating work. If there's no one available to take over some of your overload, consider your options. One option may be to hire part-time help.*
- *Post for another position within the company.*
- *Update your resume. It may be that try as you may, it's time to move on.*

Cultivate Your Tolerance for Change

Life is about change, and since it's predicted that in the next 10 years we'll see more change than in the past 20, you'd better decide today to develop a high tolerance for it. You can let the waves of change knock you down, or you can adapt to them. (It's a no-brainer choice, isn't it?)

A Paradox

The more things change, the more they stay the same. (Attributed to Alphonse Karr, 1849, originally written in French.)

I'd be totally remiss if I didn't note that while you're well advised to embrace change because change is inevitable, another truth is the one quoted above. *The more things change, the more they stay the same.* Monsieur Karr expressed this sentiment a long time ago, but it continues to be a valid statement.

Your finely honed basic skills are valuable. You probably learned to be an excellent listener, and being a superb listener is basic to doing your job well. The fact that you now schedule appointments using an electronic calendar, as well as a paper calendar, doesn't negate the fact that you must listen carefully to your boss when he asks you to set up a meeting. You must listen to learn who should be included at that meeting, how large the meeting room should be and so forth.

I've been speaking since 1990, and I still work at the basics. I have a set of steps to go through to make sure the room is ready (e.g., adequate lighting, comfortably appointed) and the equipment is working properly. I still look for new and better ways to work the stage. I look for ways to ice the cake! I embrace what works well and discard what doesn't work well.

Illustration

At the start of a three-hour session, I ask my audience if two 10-minute breaks will be sufficient to accommodate monitoring telephone messages and taking care of personal needs. People usually agree. Then I ask everyone to disable cell phones and focus! I worked as an administrative assistant for almost 20 years and know how much can be achieved when a person is able to focus, focus, focus! I announce to attendees that if one of them is needed to handle an emergency, someone in the front office will contact us.

I have discovered that simply saying, "Please turn off cell phones" doesn't enable people to be as relaxed as when I announce two scheduled breaks and a contingency plan in case of emergency.

Years ago, people weren't electronically tethered to the outside world and constantly on call. By being clear about when people can call in for messages, there is less restlessness and fidgeting in the room. People ask excellent questions and make valuable comments and stay focused! This small change enables me to give people a better chance to benefit from their time spent with me. *The announcement would be worthless if I weren't prepared to deliver a valuable session. That's basic.*

Most of the things you do well now will continue to serve you as you move toward becoming or remaining an *inner circle* assis-

tant. But that's not all there is. The times force us to focus on en-
hancements!

CHAPTER 3

WHAT DOES IT MEAN TO YOU?

As soon as you adapt a new way of looking at this profession and looking at yourself, you'll quickly find ways to become more valuable to your boss and your company. You probably won't sit there and wait to be told what to do; you'll be an initiator.

Eventually, you'll earn more respect from everyone you encounter during the workday. Vendors, for example, will know you're not just a rubber-stamp person; they'll realize you have clout. One thing leads to the next. Once vendors view you as someone with clout, they're more likely to negotiate with you. You may become instrumental in getting goods at a better price for the company, getting deliveries faster, waiving delivery charges or arranging for 90-day billing terms as opposed to 30- to 45-day terms. The latter impacts cash flow and may result in earned interest because money remains in the company bank account longer. And this is only the beginning!

Refer to Section III, Digging Deeper/Depth and Breadth of the Job, to find your road maps. They will enable you to get your arms around this new and exciting approach to your work. You don't have to reinvent the wheel. You'll discover how to proceed based upon proven methods that have worked for others and will work for you, too. And if you're already known as an *inner circle* assistant, read that section to discover creative ways to enhance and fine-tune your performance.

And Now, the Rest of the Story…

The administrative professional's role is becoming increasingly demanding as emphasis in the workplace shifts from individual, specialized performance to multi-functional, generalized performance.

In working with thousands of office professionals across the country in various industries and government organizations, I have seen that employees are being asked to do more work, play a variety of roles, support multiple people and still maintain quality in their work. *All this means more stress.*

Stress appears in response to both negative and positive conditions. You probably don't need to be reminded that driving in heavy traffic or assisting a family member who has been diagnosed with a debilitating disease is stressful. At the same time, taking the stage and delivering a well-received speech is a satisfying experience, too, albeit stressful.

Experts tell us our bodies don't know the difference between a positive and a negative stressor. A person's heartbeat and blood pressure may elevate suddenly, and blood sugar level rises in response to any kind of stress.

It's not surprising to discover that when stress isn't managed — either by releasing it appropriately or controlling it, it can cause physical ailments, poor work performance, behavioral changes and much more.

The Good News

Although stress is unavoidable, it's manageable. Stress is different for all of us. What stresses you might not stress me and vice versa. Ultimately, I believe in self-management rather than stress management. I use the term stress management only because it's familiar to most people. But just imagine for a moment how your perspective gets you into trouble. In other words, you have a negative thought about a particular situation that causes you to feel upset. If you change your thought, through self-management, you will change your response.

- *Instead of being upset, you will manage the situation.*
- *Instead of feeling hurt, you will try to understand people's actions and get to the source of the problem.*
- *Instead of feeling angry about something your team leader said, you will assertively approach her and open lines of communication.*
- *Instead of insisting that something can't be done and feeling overwhelmed by it, you will delegate the work.*
- *Instead of scheduling a meeting a week later than you prefer because all conference rooms are booked, you'll hold the meeting off site at the preferred time.*

And so it goes.

Who, Me?

Sometimes you don't even realize you're under stress. Maybe you feel things are going along fine but are just a little hectic. You may deny to others that you are *stressed.* You may even believe that you are managing all the chaos in your personal and professional life well. If you are experiencing any of the symptoms listed on the next page and do not normally experience them, it could be an indication that you are under stress, but you don't realize it or don't want to admit it. In order to take steps to minimize stress, you must first know how to recognize it.

There are four categories of stress indicators: emotional, mental, physical and behavioral.

Mental	Physical	Emotional	Behavioral
Poor judgment	Fatigue	Irritability	Sudden change in work habits
Unable to concentrate on tasks	Nervousness	Develop phobias	Easily startled by small sounds
Illogical thinking	Restlessness	Depression	Insomnia
Tendency to make more mistakes than usual	Increased breathing rate	Withdrawal	Accident prone
Performance level lower than usual	Dryness of throat	Emotional outbursts	Impulsive behavior
Extreme daydreaming	Sweaty palms	Overpowering urge to cry, run or retreat	Overeating or loss of appetite
Acting out of sorts	Cold hands and feet	Frequent hostile feelings	Increased smoking
Decrease in creative risk taking	Sudden change in appetite	General emotional instability	Increased illness and absenteeism
	Frequent heartburn and indigestion	Unpredictable behavior	Feelings of anxiety for no apparent reason

Review this list from time to time to see if you're experiencing any of the above. It's better to get a handle on stress as early as possible before it mounts up and leads to serious physical or mental problems. You might even want to reproduce this list and post it where you can review it often. If you identify with any of these symptoms, think about the positive steps you can take to combat them.

Below you'll find a short list of positive steps and a self-scoring quiz. It's essential to point out that diet, exercise, and sufficient sleep all play a vital role in a person's overall well being. Don't neglect to check with your physician, nutritionist, personal trainer or other health expert for information and support. (You may want to check bookstore shelves and the library for stress-management book titles that interest you. There's no shortage of how-to books on this topic.)

POSITIVE STEPS THAT HELP MINIMIZE STRESS

After each step, choose which of the following statements is most accurate for you.

- *Do nothing that will require you to tell a lie.*
  1) It's okay to tell little white lies.
  2) I expect others to lie to me.
  3) I feel sneaky if I tell a lie.

If you select #3 as most accurate, you certainly don't want to do something that will require you to tell a lie. (Some adjectives for sneaky include mean, shifty and underhanded.) These less-than-admirable self-accusations would render most people stressed. If you select #1 or #2 as most accurate, *doing nothing that will require you to tell a lie* is still a good rule of thumb.

- *Learn to live one day at a time.*
  1) It's better to focus on the moment than the entire day.
  2) I like to think big and don't agree with this statement.

3) That's easy to say but difficult to do.

If you select #3 as most accurate, it may interest you to know that many people consider obtaining this goal a lifetime pursuit. They continually strive to adapt this modus operandi. If you select one of the other numbers as most accurate, by all means, have it your way. No sense trying to fit a square peg into a round hole. That would be stressful!

- *Start saying no more often.*
    1) It's easier to make promises and not keep them.
    2) I figure if I make the effort, I can get the job done.
    3) I don't like to disappoint people by saying no.

If you select #1, you either go out of your way to feel stressful or you left your ethical behavior in the closet! In time, "undependable" is a label you'll merit. That's bad for your career and a stalled career may stress you. As to the other choices, both are nice-gal thoughts. Still, there are only so many hours in the day. Watch out; stress is probably lurking around the bend.

- *Get up 15 minutes earlier every day.*
    1) I need my sleep.
    2) I enjoy having 15 minutes for myself.
    3) I never miss this sleep and am always glad for the extra time.

If you insist on #1 as most accurate, did you consider going to bed earlier? Having more preparation time before you leave for work is virtually a boon to well-being. Since most busy people desire more hours in the day, settling for 15 extra minutes is better than nothing!

- *Be prepared to wait and have something to read for when you do.*
    1) I get frustrated when people don't keep appointments promptly.

2) I can't read and concentrate on something else when I'm waiting. I focus on what I'm waiting to do.

3) I think it's important to have quiet time and not fill every waking moment with action. Reading can be an action, too.

If you believe #3 is the most accurate statement, good for you. Many people prefer busywork to solitude. As for numbers 1 and 2, I sympathize with you. I prize punctuality and will probably have to accept that I'm going to be stressed by this one. You can't win them all!

- *Create order out of chaos.*
    1) That's easy. I do it all the time.
    2) I tell myself that chaos is a kind of order and don't permit it to bother me.
    3) Why?

If you select #3 because you don't understand the reason for this suggestion, I suggest you consider how you would feel on the stock market floor when trading is in high gear and the mood is fast-paced and competitive. Unless you work there, I think you may want to flee the room. For most mortals, chaos represents stress times two. If you opt for # 1 or #2, I salute you.

- *Do something that will improve your appearance.*
    1) I'm exercising three times a week.
    2) I'm working with my sister to update my wardrobe. My sister is a designer.
    3) I'm budgeting more money for professional grooming services.

Anything you select as the most accurate answer in this group is a winner!

- *Allow yourself time every day for quiet and introspection.*

1) I spend 10 minutes at the end of the business day to re-flect upon achievements.
2) I read one self-improvement book a month.
3) I kick off my shoes and enjoy quiet time with a bever-age before dinner.

The quiet time that any of these three actions offer is welcome. But introspection refers to self-examination, and although it's ad-mirable to read self-improvement books, it's not the same thing. As for listing achievements, that's deceptive. No one could argue with the feel-good results you would enjoy, but that's different than asking "Who am I?" and "What do I want?" etc.

- *Take care of unpleasant tasks early in the day and get them over with.*
    1) I save unpleasant tasks for handling on Wednesdays.
    2) I make sure I'm fortified with coffee and have read the comic strips.
    3) I'm so happy to be gainfully employed in a job I enjoy, I don't think of tasks as unpleasant.

These three statements remind us that one woman's meat is another woman's poison. You're well advised to adapt sugges-tions that work best for you, but don't close the door on other methods for achieving goals.

There's More...

- *Learn the negative aspects that go with your job. Can you change them or do you need to accept them? (Remember, there's another op-tion; you can walk away.)*
- *Set up a daily activity to renew your attitude. Many people find that physical exercise is just what the doctor ordered. On cold winter days, walk up and down the staircases. When you have lunch or a coffee break on balmy days, step outside and take a brisk walk around the building. Or get thee to the company gym.*

- *Surround yourself with positive people and reading materials. Find something or someone to make you laugh, smile or just feel happy. Motivational sayings can do the trick. Keep a small book in a desk drawer and take one a day, as needed!*
- *Take a mental break. (This isn't the same as a breakdown!) Find something to focus on that's unrelated to the tasks you're handling. Refresh for a few moments by leaving those cares behind. You'll probably be able to work more efficiently when you return to them.*

Add to this list when you find something more that enables you to minimize stress.

On the next page is another exercise you may find revealing. Remember, this is a for-your-eyes-only evaluation. Be candid. No one will see this unless you decide to share it.

EVALUATING WORK STRESS

Activity: How often are you confronted with the following job realities?

Frequency Scale

	5 Always	4 Often	3 Some- times	2 Rarely	1 Never
Unclear expectations from my manager					
Difference of opinion with superiors					
Demands of others for my time					
Overqualified for job					
Underqualified for job					
Little opportunity to use my knowledge and creativity					
Work assignments are not meaningful					
Too much to do in too little time					
Multiple changes within the organization					
Conflict with coworkers					
Lack of appreciation from immediate supervisor					
Work more than 40 hours per week					

List your top three work-related stressors in order of priority. You can refer to the list above or add your own.

1) _____
2) _____
3) _____

Talk About Sharing

You don't have to share this exercise and your responses with anyone, but don't permit it to become an exercise in futility. If you enjoy open lines of communication with the executive(s) you support, you may want to reveal some of what you've identified. It's useful if you can step into a meeting with solutions to the challenges you're about to reveal. If you don't enjoy open lines of communication, why not focus on the top work-related stressors and design a plan of action? (Look at road maps in Section III. It's likely that one or more of them will make it easy for you to design a plan of action.)

Illustration

Marie is the name we'll use for another fictitious administrative assistant. Once again, this illustration is based on real-time circumstances happening in offices all over our country on a daily basis.

Marie was responsible for supporting six managers. She called a meeting with all of them to explain her realization that no matter how she tried, there was simply too much to do and too little time in which to do it.

"Here's where I can be of most assistance," she began. She went on to clarify each manager's needs and then indicated that she could fulfill each assignment with flying colors if the coordination of all six calendars and the travel planning for all six managers were delegated to others. She wound up by saying those two tasks were relatively easy to perform but very time-consuming. "I'll make arrangements to delegate these tasks today, if you approve."

- *Do you think Marie sounded like a complainer?*
- *Do you think she made them an offer they couldn't refuse?*

When she planned her presentation, she kept her eye on these two questions. She wanted the answers to be in her favor (no and yes, respectively). She also wanted her message to be clear, short and sweet.

Marie ended with a call to action. Let us suppose that when she walked out of the meeting she was able to put her checkmark in the box above marked "Rarely." She would rarely (after all, she is a practical lady and doesn't believe in "never") have too much to do and too little time to do it.

Of course, this presumes that Marie is also highly organized. Her work station is set up for efficiency. For example, she doesn't get up from her desk to walk to her printer 20 times a day. That printer is an arm's length away. (Read more about this in the road map you'll find in Section III under Office Organization.)

By the way, Marie also felt that decisions about her job were made without any input from her. She decided to save this concern for another day. She reasoned that when the six managers started to see her in a different light (because she confronted them, offered a solution and got permission to delegate tasks), they might begin to consult with her more often.

Illustration

Here's an illustration that strikes close to home. At one time, I was an administrative assistant, working all of the 40 hours a week I was hired to work. I didn't hang out at the water cooler when the executives were away from the department. But I knew that if I was truly working my full 40 hours a week and still couldn't do all that was assigned to me, something had to give. There were 45 managers with only five administrative assistants serving as support staff. I talked about all the new things I did. I mentioned how I was teaching others and so forth, but basically I was told "Sorry, we can't help you." Then a few of us put together a task analysis and presented it to management. The analysis made our point, and management subsequently hired more people!

Illustration

One executive believed an administrative assistant went overboard with her proofreading chores. She was such a slave to details that she would actually proofread documents 10 times before releasing them. The executive knew this and felt that what was normally an admirable trait, an insistence on accuracy, had become a fault.

"Enough is enough," the executive told me. "Make things happen. Move forward." He wanted me to communicate this to the assistant.

In the end, this assistant resigned from her position and everyone was happy. She was too stressed working for two managers because she just wasn't good at multitasking. She went into a job supporting one executive.

- *How many 5s do you think this assistant would check off in the box on page 27?*
- *Are you proud of her for recognizing the job wasn't a good fit and for moving on?*

She would probably benefit from reading and using the road maps in Section III, especially those under Task & Project Management. It could make a positive difference for her if the future brings more changes and she finds herself supporting more than one executive. A star performer doesn't get hung up on one thing. She knows when to take the extra steps and when not to take them.

Stepping Out of the Safety Zone Is Stressful

Price Pritchett, author of *New Work Habits for the Next Millennium*, says, "Our current work habits produce weaker results as circumstances change. The more rapid the change, and the more radical the shift, the sooner our usual approaches lose their punch.

"We have to choose between two risks. First, we can gamble on our old habits and watch our career skills gradually grow obsolete. Or we can accept the risks of the pioneer. The inventor. The explorer. The greater safety lies in choosing this second risk, even though it feels more chancy than the first."

When viewed from this perspective, it becomes clear that on the cutting edge is the place to be. Today's *inner circle* assistant:

- *Keeps up with technology by reading technical journals, talking with systems people, learning what programs coworkers use and recommend, attending classes, and just practicing and exploring techniques on her own computer.*
- *Looks for better ways to do things. Doesn't assume that the way she performs today is the most effective and efficient way. She knows that chances are there's a better, smarter way to perform. She questions her habits and uses her creativity.*

- *Expands horizons to include other departments. She's not so focused on her own area that she doesn't know about changes taking place in other departments. If something works she considers whether it's adaptable to her department's needs. If it is, she implements it or touts it to her boss.*
- *Helps break down the barriers between management and colleagues. For too many years, there has been a separation between management and employees. She rolls up her sleeves, gets involved and works next to people. She realizes that "We're all in this together."*
- *Attacks the future instead of protecting the past. Some people are working hard at keeping things status quo. These are the people who may not be in the workplace in a few years. They're fighting a lost cause. Change is underway. Market competition is tough. We're living our future today.*
- *Is willing to take risks. Yes, this is scary (stressful!) and probably one of the most difficult things you will do. However, if you don't take reasonable risks, you never know what you're really capable of doing. If you venture out and it doesn't turn out like you thought, learn from the experience. At least you'll know what the rest of the world is doing.*
- *Reads the periodicals her manager reads. Explores the Internet. (Keeps it business related when she's at work.) Is open to new ideas, concepts and trends. Finds out how other office professionals in different parts of the country do things. What about different industries and business sizes (e.g., more or less than 1,000 employees)?*
- *Takes responsibility. Doesn't wait for others to lead her down a path. Determines her goals, sets priorities and is accountable for her actions. Lives the life she wants to live. Fulfills her dreams.*

Remember:

"Champions aren't made in gyms. Champions are made from something they have deep inside them—a desire, a dream, a vision. They have to have last-minute stamina, they have to be a little faster, and they have to have the skills and the will. But the will must be stronger than the skill."

- Muhammad Ali

SECTION TWO

Some Things Never Change

CHAPTER 4

Let's Talk Basics

Guy Lombardi put it best when he said, "Be brilliant at the basics."

Today, it's not good enough to just be good at the basics. You must be brilliant at the basics. It's easy to forget some of the rules you learned years ago; and if you have been in the same position or field for many years, it's easy to get into a comfortable mode and not push for excellence. The *inner circle* assistant never rests on her laurels. She doesn't take her basics, like communication and telephone skills, for granted. The fundamentals are paramount in today's fast-paced office.

What Are the Basics?

Pause to digest the meaning of the words "skill" and "competency" and you can better understand what's meant by "the basics."

Simply stated, a skill refers to your ability to perform a function. You, for example, are probably a typist. Typing may be important to your job, but if that's all you have to offer, you probably wouldn't be reading this book! You combine numerous skills in order to be a valued employee. That combination of skills serves as your foundation. Doctors and nurses must have excellent foundation skills to be good at their jobs. Attorneys, entrepreneurs, sales people and CEOs need excellent foundation skills to excel in their careers, too. It doesn't take a rocket scientist to realize each of these people must perfect the skills required to perform their particular jobs.

But what are those core foundation skills in which you need to excel and then build upon to be a truly successful administrative professional?

What level is your performance in various skill, attitude and knowledge areas? Where do you need to grow? What are the skills, attitudes and behaviors managers seek in administrative staff?

Without enhancing current people and business skills and learning new ones, even the best administrative professionals will not be able to advance in their field or even expand their current position.

Enter the word "competency."

In the introduction to this book, I used the word competency and gave it a one-word definition—"responsibility." The following excerpts, taken from *Training and Development* magazine, offer a more complete explanation. (Please note: The magazine article is somewhat technical, so I've excerpted the essential message.)

"In the job world, competency has many meanings. Some definitions relate to the work—tasks, results and outputs. Others describe the characteristics of the people doing the work—knowledge, skills and attitudes (also values, orientations and commitments). A hybrid often mixes those two kinds of definitions into an attribute bundle.

"Human resource executives refer to knowledge, skills and attitude competencies. In this case, subject matter (such as engineering knowledge), process abilities (such as listening skills), and attitudes, values, orientations and commitments (such as integrity and achievement) are called competencies.

"They also refer to attribute bundles. A bundle of attributes or attribute bundle is a label for a collection of knowledge, skills and attitudes—or tasks, outputs and results. This hybrid form of competency typically uses such terms as leadership, problem solving and decision making."

You've probably heard the saying, "Knowledge is power." But the acquisition of knowledge is not enough. You can acquire all the knowledge necessary, but until you transfer knowledge into behavior, it's of questionable value and doesn't make you powerful.

So even when you completely agree with Guy Lombardi's admonition to be "brilliant at the basics," and even when you have the big-picture vantage point concerning what constitutes basics, you must *act* accordingly.

Don't forget the road maps in Section III are designed to help you achieve your goals. They focus on the twelve Key Competencies mentioned earlier:

TWELVE KEY COMPETENCIES

1. Appointment Coordination
2. Manager Support
3. Managing Office Technology
4. Meeting Preparation & Coordination
5. Office Communication
6. Office Organization
7. Problem Solving
8. Professional Behavior & Image
9. Professional Development
10. Supporting Multiple Managers
11. Task & Project Management
12. Time Management

Right now, however, we'll review basics by examining a few scenarios. Each scenario begins with words of wisdom that pay homage to actions that are important to today's *inner circle* assistant.

Illustration

- *Making others feel good about themselves and supporting their goals isn't a later-day, high-tech innovation.*
  It's what a good leader does.

The *inner circle* assistant calls upon basic leadership skills daily. For example, she keeps cool under pressure. She knows that when you feel pressured, you tend not to think as clearly and may respond to situations and people in a way that you later regret.

She reasons that she's only one person with only so many hours in a day. If something doesn't get done today, it will be done tomorrow.

In our "do it/fax it today" society, people feel like they have to get all their work done now. What is the worst that will happen if you can't get that project finished today or you can't get that letter out today? In most cases, everyone can live with the consequences.

A Laundry List

Be known as an action person. Do what you say you'll do. (This is so simple, yet most people don't do it.) If you realize you can't follow through on something you said you would do, acknowledge it as soon as possible and explain to others why you can't. Just don't make a habit of not fulfilling your commitments. Review your goals regularly.

Take charge. People respond more positively when you clearly communicate your needs and establish deadlines while still respecting their needs. Taking charge also means responding to negative behavior rather than letting people get away with inappropriate actions. Buckle down to accomplish unpleasant or difficult tasks without delay.

This is quite a laundry list, and you could probably add to it! In addition to all the other times leadership skills come to your aid in the workplace, they certainly underscore success when you want to make others feel good about themselves and support their goals.

There's nothing new here except maybe a new way of looking at leadership and what it achieves. The payoff is so rewarding that brushing up on leadership basics from time to time is a good habit to cultivate.

A SHORT STORY (The administrative assistant is a figment of my imagination, but the leadership principles are factual!)

Kelly walked into the conference room and surprised two employees who were reading romance novels when they should have been collating and inserting materials in binders. The materials were to be used as handouts when her boss addressed prospective investors at a meeting scheduled for Tuesday, which was the following day.

"What's the problem?" she asked. "Did you run out of fasteners? Did you send someone to the supply room to get more of them?"

The employees were clearly embarrassed. "We're just taking a break," one woman replied. "The fasteners hurt our fingers."

Kelly explained that the handouts were needed for the next day. "Let's see if there's a better way to secure the papers," she offered. She left the room briefly and returned with a rubber thumb protector. The employees looked wary.

"I can't use that," one woman said. "It will ruin my manicure."

Kelly ignored the comment and proceeded to fasten materials using the thumb protector. "I'll try it without the protector, too," she announced and did just that.

"I think it's just as easy to do the job without the thumb protector," she said. One woman returned to the job. The woman who mentioned her manicure said, "I don't want to do this."

Kelly knew the employee well and was surprised by her lack of cooperation. "I'm sorry you feel that way, Grace. Mr. Belmont is depending on us to have these binders ready for his meeting tomorrow." Grace was silent. "I'll take your place, Grace," Kelly announced. "You can return to your desk work."

When Grace left the room, the other employee said to Kelly, "I'm glad you didn't get angry. Grace's dog died yesterday, and she's a mess."

Leadership Basics

- *Don't stray from the mission.*
- *Don't tolerate unacceptable behavior.*
- *Don't shy away from conflict.*

And Kelly did something more. She relied upon past experience with Grace and gave her the benefit of the doubt. She quickly discovered the reason for Grace's uncooperative manner, and she won points with the other employee, too. The fact that she stepped in for Grace made a statement. (This is important work, and we're all in this together.) There's a good chance that both employees were appreciative of Kelly's response. And the incident passed without causing harm. Kelly is probably an *inner circle* assistant using top-notch leadership skills every day and varying skill sets to meet specific goals.

- *You may already manipulate challenging Computer Aided Design programs with ease and perform all kinds of impressive office tasks, but if you ever shut yourself off from learning, you'll be stuck out in left field.*

Uncover Great Ideas by Taking Off Your Blinders

When you're frequently on the lookout for better ways to do things, it's as though you're wearing a sign that says, "I'm open for business!"

Great ideas are hard to come by, but often, they're right under our noses. Great ideas abound in the work place. Discovering them is simply a matter of making unique connections and running with a seemingly ordinary idea that no one else knows is great. Here are two ways to sharpen your ability to recognize great ideas:

- *Ideas come from small places. Richard Trayford was only killing time between jobs when he took a position with a bicycle messenger service. But it was there that he generated the idea that launched his multimillion-dollar business, Citipost. The same-day messenger service offered overnight delivery anywhere in the city for $1 as a promotion to its regular service. Trayford used the promotion idea to start his own business. He created a bicycle messenger service that delivered overnight anywhere in the city for just $1. Eight years later, the company posted $20 million in revenues and had expanded around the globe.*

- *Complaints can generate ideas. Take every complaint seriously. As a customer service rule, this is a given. But few people look at complaints within the organization as idea generators. Steve Utter did. His employees kept complaining about the heat in the Arizona summers. It was depressing productivity at his Phoenix-based construction company. He was trying to figure out a solution when he saw a fog nozzle used by gardeners to spread insecticide in a fine mist. His idea for a cooling mister was born. Misty Mate is a fanny-pack-sized water supply that straps to the waist with a flexible tube that clips to the shirt collar. Anytime the heat gets unbearable, workers can find relief with a mist of water.*

A FILL-IN QUIZ

You may want to make a copy of this page if you don't want to write in this book! Or number a clean sheet of paper and put your answers on the paper next to the number that corresponds to one in the book.

1. It's not uncommon for adults to ask children, "What did you learn at school today?" If someone asked me what I learned at work today, here's how I would answer:_____

    _____

    _____

2. Ron Richardson, training director for Drummond Company, tells employees, "You should ask yourself two questions at the end of each day.
    1) What did I do today to help my department or organization?
    2) What did I do today to add to my toolbox?"

    I wonder if Mr. Richardson realizes that when employees ask themselves question #1, they're learning how valuable they are (or aren't) to Drummond. If you asked yourself that question for the last three business days, what would your answers be?

    1) _____

    _____

    _____

    2) _____

    _____

    _____

3) _____

   _____

   _____

3. The last classroom course I took was entitled,

_____

_____. If I can't remember the last classroom course I took, it's time to check out adult education courses at schools in my community. In either case, I could really use some updating on computer programs, accounting principles, creative writing, business communications,

_____

_____.

4. Magazines and other publications are routed to me in the office, and I scan or read them. I also subscribe to publications at home. I must vary what I read so that I expose myself to different information and different points of view. I will drop my subscription to

_____

when it expires and take a subscription to

_____.

5. When I attend business luncheons or participate in seminars, I (do/don't [circle one]) sit with people I know. That's because (Please circle one of the following statements): a) I learn more when I interact with people I don't know. b) That's because it gives us an opportunity to know one another better. Now, after circling the statement that applies better to you, consider whether the other statement option has merit. If it does, you may want to change your approach next chance you get.

There are many approaches to being a lifelong student. The *inner circle* assistant is always on the lookout for learning something new.

- *You may think out of the box to find solutions to problems and encourage others to do the same, but if you aren't inclined to reserve judgment while you gather the facts, you may become the problem.*

It's easy to rush to judgment. You may, for example, step into the cafeteria and see four employees in a huddle, whispering. A moment after you enter the room, one of them signals the others to disperse. *I bet they're talking about me.* You recently had liposuction performed on your midsection and believe that's the stimulus for gossip. Suddenly, the vice president of sales bumps into you and shakes you out of your reverie. "Only one more week of cafeteria food," he quips. "Starting next week, this man is retired!" You smile but continue to think about *the gossips.* Later, you realize that you and the vice president entered the cafeteria at almost the same moment. Employees probably dispersed when they saw him. He's well liked, and people were making plans to buy a gift for him as he retires. (*Oops! You initially came to the wrong conclusion.*)

Activity: A person's responses are often dictated by her general attitude. Take a moment to indicate your opinions about attitude by placing an X in the appropriate box. Of course, your attitude impacts almost everything you do and will be spotlighted more than once in this book.

Agree	Not Sure	Dis- agree		
☐	☐	☐	My attitude is changeable.	
☐	☐	☐	The quality of work I produce varies depending on my attitude.	
☐	☐	☐	I don't have any choice but to get upset with difficult people.	
☐	☐	☐	I don't need to do anything to keep myself upbeat. It will just happen.	
☐	☐	☐	My attitude needs to be handled gently.	
☐	☐	☐	I have ultimate control of my attitude.	
☐	☐	☐	I should always express exactly how I feel.	
☐	☐	☐	Setting and achieving goals does not affect attitude.	
☐	☐	☐	I don't see any benefit when criticized about my work.	
☐	☐	☐	Fear is good. It lets me know my limits.	

SCORE: When you're upbeat, you're less likely to make false assumptions. If you don't think you need to work at staying upbeat, think again. Review all your responses in light of rushing to judgment. Pay special attention to the statements about which you indicated you were not sure. More than three Not Sure responses act like a red flag. Stop. Think. If, for example, you're not sure about whether you should always express exactly how you feel, shake off indecision. It's always prudent to think before you speak. This little chart and few observations are designed to act like cactus barbs; they're intended to make you sit up and take notice of your response behavior. If you rush to judgment prior to obtaining all related information, you'll be banished to the proverbial waiting room. There you'll remain and never step through the door marked *inner circle* assistant. It may help to think of yourself as being stuck in the waiting room when an incident unfolds that makes your temperature rise. If this mental picture enables you to stave off rushing to judgment, it's a winner.

- *It's necessary to hold your emotions in check when faced with challenges. Maintaining your cool has always been and still is important. The* inner circle *assistant knows that good enough is seldom enough.*

If 99.9 percent were good enough then . . .

- *12 newborns would be given to the wrong parents daily.*
- *144,500 mismatched pairs of shoes would be shipped per year.*
- *18,322 pieces of mail would be mishandled per hour.*
- *The IRS would lose 2,000,000 documents this year.*
- *2.5 million books would be shipped with the wrong covers.*
- *Two planes landing at Chicago's O'Hare Airport would be unsafe every day.*
- *315 entries in Webster's Dictionary would be misspelled.*
- *20,000 incorrect drug prescriptions would be written.*
- *880,000 credit cards in circulation would have incorrect cardholder information on their magnetic strips.*
- *103,260 income tax returns would be processed incorrectly during the year.*
- *291 pacemaker operations would be performed incorrectly.*

- *3,056 copies of the* Wall Street Journal *would be missing one of three sections.*

These statistics make an interesting case for keeping your cool. But alas, you're only human, and although you're not going to run the white flag of surrender up the pole, you may rely upon another basic—the fine art of delegation.

Delegating vs. Dumping

There's a difference between dumping and delegating. Dumping usually happens impulsively.

Successful delegating is dependent upon the careful selection of the right person whose skills and strength are matched to the needs of the task at hand. It also means giving the person you've chosen the authority to get the job done and to encourage independent action. When delegating, keep these tips in mind:

- *Timing is crucial. Try to distribute assignments equally to all involved in helping you complete the project or task. Be sensitive to the workload of others.*
- *Delegate but stay in control. Do so by sticking to a plan for following up on the person's performance.*
- *Believe what people tell you. Learn to accept what others tell you, even if the news is unpleasant or conflicts with your opinions. (Remember — you can't do it all yourself.)*
- *Stand back. Don't try to know every detail of the operation at every moment.*
- *If the result is disappointing, examine the process. Discuss what went wrong. Explore what might have led to a different, better result.*

You can probably add to this list, too. Basic delegation skills can save the day and help the *inner circle* assistant keep her cool. It's a clever way of crying for help and getting help. Essentially, the cry is silent. No one need ever know that for a little while,

50

your emotions were unleashed and flying off in too many diverse directions.

A SHORT STORY: (Again, the administrative assistant is not an actual person but a composite of so many wonderful administrative professionals I have known. And again, the delegation principles are rock solid.)

Vivian was a single mom who worked full time. She loved her job and considered herself to be a star achiever. In May, Vivian and her teenage daughters moved miles away from their cheery townhouse to live with Vivian's dad, who was now too frail to be living on his own. Her dad's house was new and large enough to accommodate them all comfortably. Her daughters were closer to their high school and liked the fact they could stay late for extracurricular activities without worrying about transportation, since they could walk home. Her daughters and her dad adjusted to the new living arrangements almost immediately. But Vivian couldn't say the same. She had no idea where to go to get the car fixed, etc. And she missed the daily chats with a former neighbor who was a trusted confidant. She recognized she was embarking on a period of adjustment.

When her boss announced that the company was about to sell off her division, she was aware of blinking back tears. The workload over the next few weeks seemed excessive. Finally, Vivian announced to her boss that she was engaging two temporary workers to assist with the extra auditing and reporting that was necessary to support the sale. She micromanaged each temporary employee for the first two weeks, and when she was satisfied that they could be given more rope, she gave it to them. She didn't stop there. At home, she asked her daughters for help. "I would rather not raid the bank account to pay for cleaning help," she explained. "You'll have to count me out for a few months. I'll shop and cook, as usual, but you girls will have to handle the cleaning. Can you do it?" Vivian delegated tasks on several levels.

By the time the division was sold and she was asked to stay on with her boss to work for the new owner, she had regained her balance. She was ready to tackle a Superwoman mode of operation once again. Her emphasis on maintaining her cool at all times always came to her rescue. She may not always continue to rely upon delegating tasks to attain a goal, but it's certainly a viable option.

- *You're bombarded by information from varied sources on a daily basis. Still, how can you anticipate emerging trends and otherwise read your company's future unless you focus, focus and focus?*
- *Respecting confidences and performing ethically is basic to any inner circle administrative professional's modus operandi. Even when lines are easily blurred in this complicated business environment, personal integrity is highly valued.*
- *Displaying tact, creativity and simply being a nice person are attributes that must remain no matter how many corks you're keeping underwater at the same time.*

CHAPTER 5

Not Just Another Pretty Face
(or Brains—Who Needs Them?)

For the first time in history, the administrative professional's job description hints at full engagement of cognitive powers. Sure, it takes brains to learn tasks such as changing ink cylinders in copy machines, but when the job description includes identifying goals for the coming year; meshing them with your executive's goals and department and organization goals; being prepared to track progress at specific intervals; and being accountable for success or lack thereof, it's easy to tell this is not a job for dummies!

You're not a puppet, and someone else is not pulling the strings. You're in charge. You have power. And if you're to attain the *inner circle* assistant spot and maintain it, your intellect plays a large part in your success. So if the best career advice you've received so far is to dress for success, get ready to think bigger. And "think" is the operating word.

Illustration

I was working with a member of the governor's cabinet in Louisville, Kentucky. Her calendar was always jammed with appointments. Nothing could be done about that, but she believed there must be a better way to operate. She called me for help.

"My administrative assistant uses the latest electronic calendar to schedule appointments," she explained. I thought, "It may be that the administrative assistant's only criteria are to fill slots."

I asked the administrative assistant to print out the previous week's appointments. I told her we would treat one hour of our day as though it were a single calendar day. My goal was to review a week in seven hours. (Please note: We didn't examine a five-day workweek since the governor frequently attended weekend functions.) Then, the administrative assistant and I literally traveled to each appointment location. She immediately saw that her boss was on the go each day of the week.

"How do you feel?" I asked at the end of our seven hours (representing seven days).

"Exhausted," she replied.

"By the end of the week, it must be difficult to be efficient," I added. "And you didn't have time to make phone calls, sign papers or answer e-mail."

This administrative assistant was a capable person but unaccustomed to thinking about the consequences of her actions. Instead of thinking about each calendar entry she made, she did, in fact, simply fill in the slots.

"You have a lot of power," I told her.

She was silent for a moment and then responded, "I really pull my bosses strings, don't I?"

From that day forward she applied these rules:
- *If there are two consecutive days with back-to-back appointments, the third day should be appointment free.*
- *Back-to-back appointments must be logistically sound. If, for example, there's one meeting in the East Wing and another across the campus, a reasonable interval between appointments is essential. (My boss needs to get from one place to the next without feeling*

stressed. She must have free time to attend to personal needs and free time to contact the office for messages.)

- *Lunch and personal work time will be put on each day's calendar. They take precedence over any other appointment. It will take an emergency of considerable proportions for me to deviate from this rule.*

I complimented her when she sent me a printed copy of her new rules. "How do you decide which appointments take priority?" I asked.

"I never thought of that," she responded.

Apparently, she was not yet fully accustomed to engaging the complete spectrum of her cognitive powers.

I could almost hear her blush over the telephone.

"May I call you when I have my new plan of action?" she inquired.

You know that I said, "Yes, please do."

Unlocking the Internal Dragon

This administrative assistant didn't realize it at the time, but she was on the verge of being introduced to her Internal Dragon. I had seen this happen before, and I'm always delighted when this particular Dragon arrives on the scene.

It's my way of identifying a person's new awareness of her power. The individual embraces flexibility instead of avoiding it. The change comes complete with a burst of energy that begs to be translated into positive actions. The administrative assistant *actively* listens to people and becomes more assertive. She starts to look at problem solving in a new way. For example, here's a look at how to handle scheduling and meetings that knocks the socks off the ordinary approach:

1. Look at the bigger picture. That could include the next week, the next month and perhaps the first quarter of the year. You'll make that decision based upon all that you know about your company and the executives you support (e.g., the Christmas season puts heavy demands on everyone, so avoid scheduling meetings if possible).

2. Do more up-front work. For example, you should know why the meeting is being called. What's the goal?

3. When your boss needs to meet with three executives but one is traveling, what then? Should you set up a conference call meeting? Should you ask this executive's administrative assistant to attend in his place? (If you did your up-front work, you're better able to find a solution to the challenge.)

4. Know what your executive can handle. If he has just come in from a different time zone, don't schedule an important appointment for him. (Executives frequently tell me, "I've been sleeping poorly in hotels and haven't eaten well. The last thing I need to come home to is a heavy meeting.")

5. Take the initiative. If your executive is running a fever, cancel meetings scheduled for that day.

6. Get strict with your gate-keeping tasks when the executive you support needs time to prepare and reflect before he conducts or attends a meeting. In other words, give him space.

7. If your executive isn't a morning person, don't schedule early-morning meetings. She may need to drink her coffee, read e-mails or simply wake up first!

8. Don't always do what the boss says you should do. Does this one surprise you? You'll have to muster your courage and probably follow this advice only on rare occasions. But when something seems wrong, out of order, possibly detrimental to your boss (like scheduling a meeting close to the time he must leave for the airport), don't do it!

Do you see what happens when your internal Dragon comes out to play? It's probably safe to say that the typical administrative assistant would *never* employ all these strategies. She wouldn't wield her power, even though she has power. What good is it if you don't use it?

Get Organized!

"Don't agonize, organize." (Attributed to Florynce Kennedy, lawyer and writer, 1916–2000.)

I enthusiastically favor being organized and applaud Ms. Kennedy's observation! That's because when you're organized you:
- *Find things faster.*
- *Use time more effectively.*
- *Look professional.*
- *Will have necessary supplies available.*

Office organization is a Key Competency discussed later in the book. I introduce it briefly now to demonstrate that when the Internal Dragon propels you forward and you find yourself more involved, it's possible to have both the time and the wherewithal to cope with new demands.

An Insider's View

Being organized is one of five skills most requested by managers and employers across the country. (The others are telephone, computer, time management and communication skills.)

Here's What Happens When You Are:

Not Organized	Organized
Waste time	Use time more effectively
Create re-work	Do things right the first time
Make errors	Reduce errors
Add stress	Reduce stress
Keep others from doing their work	Provide good customer service
Don't have necessary materials	Look professional
	Have necessary supplies on hand

As you can see from the chart above, many negative things happen when you're not organized. You might think you don't have time to organize your work area and supplies, that you have just enough time in a day to get your work done. Look to the future. Don't think you don't have the time today. By making time now to get organized, you will save yourself time in the future. If your days are too hectic, stay after work one night or go in on a Saturday. In the long run, you will save yourself hours of time, frustration and stress.

Tips That Tell the Tale

Let's get specific so that you can appreciate this is not pie-in-the-sky thinking. You'll find a more complete road map later in the book, but these few tips will probably provide you with at least one "A-ha" moment. As a matter of fact, chances are good you're not applying any of these strategies. Adapt them and make a positive difference. You don't need to take my word for it. Prove it to yourself.

1) Be careful that your workspace does not become storage space.

Make it a place of action. Don't hold onto files and other materials that are used infrequently. Find another area to store them. If your file cabinets are full, examine each file and ask yourself, "Am I storing things we don't need anymore?" If so, either send them to the shredder or pack them off to central storage. Or you may need more storage space. That usually comes complete with the need for an excellent system to help categorize files. No sense saving anything if you don't know you have it and don't know how to retrieve it. This could be an excellent time to question company policy on record retention. Some records must be saved to comply with government regulations. But most records don't need to be saved forever. If the company doesn't have a record retention policy, you may want to start the ball rolling to establish one.

2) Place the items you most frequently use closest to you.

Analyze your activities. Decide which items are used the most and place them in an easy-to-reach spot. You might think it only takes 30 seconds to get an item, but add up the number of times you do that in a day and see how much time you can save. It's a valuable and eye-opening exercise to perform.

3) A messy desk signals lack of control and focus.

Some people assume that if they don't have papers spread all over their desks, others won't think they're busy. It actually sends a message of not being organized or focused; it looks like you don't know what's going on. In some instances, people question whether you are losing things.

Most importantly, the star maintains a question mark in her subconscious, not a period. "How can we do it better?"

While you're questioning, ask yourself if there are other resources you can use. The *inner circle* assistant works at not having to reinvent the wheel.

Illustration

Dawn and I were searching on the Internet for something about meetings when we came across a fabulous planning guide for meeting executives. It included everything one would need to have to operate a big meeting or conference. It contained samples of every imaginable check-off list. We purchased the guide!

If you're not good at organizing, don't despair. Remember that we're talking about the *inner circle* assistant and how she doesn't let anything stop her from making progress! You'll want to be aware that some people aren't good at organizing, and it's not their fault! It has to do with their brains. A so-called right-brained person, one who is typically gifted in the arts, may need assistance to get organized. Afterward, however, it's important that this individual maintain the arrangement. The *inner circle* assistant will stretch to compensate for her gap areas where the ordinary I'm-just-here-to-do-my-job assistant will say, "I don't like to do that. I don't want to do that. It's not my job. I just want to do what I want to do."

The *best of the best* will say, "I get it! I understand the impact it has on my job to be organized. Even if I don't like to do this, I'm going to have to make a conscious effort to keep at it. "

Illustration

There are times when I've printed 10 e-mails and stacked them because I was leaving to attend a meeting. But as soon as I returned, I placed them where they belong. It's all based upon *Action That Needs to Be Taken*. In my office, everything fits into one of four categories: To Do, Follow Up, To Call or Call Me Back.

Amanda, another *fictional* administrative assistant, adapted my suggestions, setting up four trays and labeling them To Do, Follow Up, To Call and, for her own customized purposes, Mr. Curtis. (Reader, take note: Mr. Curtis isn't an *Action That Needs to Be Taken* label.)

She was enjoying her newly organized days and feeling on top of things until a few weeks passed. She was spending a lot of time going through the stack of papers that accumulated in the Mr. Curtis tray. As a matter of fact, she had begun to leave some papers over at the end of the day, planning to designate Fridays as the day to sort them. One day, I called Amanda to inquire how she was doing. When she mentioned that things were no better than before, we discussed her strategies. Later in the month we spoke again, and Amanda was much happier.

"I only maintain Action Trays," she told me. "And I don't save anything for sorting. I place everything as quickly as possible throughout the workday. If that's impossible, I come to the office a few minutes early the following day just to sort papers."

I told Amanda that when I'm traveling I often bring home a stack of papers and that placing each paper in one of my four trays is a high priority when I return to my office.

Learn From the Best

Most of the things I learned about being a topnotch performer I learned from the topnotch executives for whom I worked.

When you have a boss who is ready to teach you about the business, one who is willing to be your mentor, soak it up! Pardon my being so direct, but this takes *brains*.

Use your head and you'll find you shift the way you think, the way you perform. You will be rewarded. Everyone thinks first about money, and that's a fine reward. But what about personal satisfaction? Most of the administrative assistants I meet want work that has meat! When you shift your thinking and change your attitude, doors open, and you get more challenging and interesting work to do.

As you learn from the best, you'll become:
- *Process oriented as opposed to task oriented.*
- *Interested in the value and consequences of your actions.*
- *Concerned about the bottom line.*
- *Vitally aware of the scope of the business.*
- *Aware that your time has a dollar value (i.e., time is money).*
- *Cognizant that you are one of "them." Prior to this time, you thought of management as "them" and you and your coworkers as "us."*
- *Someone who changes her behavior by repeated exposure to these new ideas, concepts, principles.*

And… You will stop thinking like a secretary!

This isn't meant to be insulting; this is meant to be eye-opening. For example:

SECRETARY says: I would dress better if they paid me more.
YOU comment: Why not do it now?

SECRETARY says: I can only attend one seminar a year.
YOU comment: I should attend seminars that will enable me to perform more skillfully. I'll bring all pertinent opportunities to my manager's attention for discussion.

SECRETARY says: I'll give the company newsletter editor my favorite cheesecake recipe for the June issue.
YOU comment: Executives don't do that! I won't do things that hurt my image. I'll save that recipe for the church newsletter editor.

SECRETARY says: Let me get my steno pad or legal pad and take it to the meeting.
YOU comment: If I walk into the meeting with a pad in hand, without opening my mouth, I'm announcing to everyone assembled, "I'm a secretary." As for me, I'm taking my briefcase to the meeting.

SECRETARY says: Oh, good. I can wear Capri pants and sandals to attend Joan's seminar.
YOU comment: We're going to a business function, not a picnic. My personal appearance helps me earn respect from others.

I say, "Good for *you!*"

Please see the back of this book for a World-Class Administrative Assistant High-Level Boot Camp discount coupon. There's an I READ JOAN'S BOOK certificate request form at the back of the book, too. You're entitled to receive this from Office Dynamics, Ltd. and display it or ask that it be added to your employee file. The certificate states that the administrative professional who reads, understands and uses most of the information in Joan's book is grooming herself for a position in the *inner circle*.

CHAPTER 6

Know Thyself:
Internal vs. External Wiring

You may be familiar with the terms "introvert" and "extrovert." The popular conception of an introvert is mired in negativity. Someone who is quiet or uncommunicative is frequently labeled an introvert and problematic.

For our purposes, we'll use the terms "internal" and "external." The person who prefers to process information internally isn't thought of as problematic; it's understood that he or she is simply wired differently from a friend or colleague who is outgoing, or external. Interestingly, an internal person is frequently outgoing. The difference is that that individual rejoices when he or she can slip away from the crowd and think in peace.

Since the *inner circle* assistant is a thinker and relies heavily on cognitive powers, it helps to know more about yourself and whether you're an internal or external type. The following explanations are not scientific and are based primarily upon my observations.

The Internally Focused Person

It's easier for the internal person to stay on track because that person doesn't need to socialize in the office. Sure, she socializes because she doesn't wish to be ostracized or perceived as unfriendly. But she is perfectly content left alone. On the whole, the internally focused person grows weary when dealing with others and needs time alone to recharge.

The Externally Focused Person

This person verbalizes what she is thinking. When she says something aloud to a coworker, she may also be explaining it to herself! She feels energized by people and would feel cut off and unhappy if she had to work quietly without interacting with others. People with whom she communicates don't need to be in the room. They may, in fact, be on the telephone.

This all goes to show that labels can be misleading. It may surprise you to know that I personally have a strong preference for the internal way of operating, even though most folks think of a speaker and trainer as an extrovert.

For example, in an office setting, I can be very much into my own work. When my children were young and I was writing, there were times when one of them would tell me something that didn't register.

"Where's Brian?" my husband would ask at the end of the day, inquiring into our son's whereabouts. Now Brian had told me his plans earlier, but he did so while my concentration was riveted to my work. So I couldn't answer my husband's question!

(If you want to know more about the concept of introverts and extroverts, it goes back to the 1920s and the psychologist Carl Jung. Mine is not a scientific attempt to explain all the nuances, but only an FYI. The more you know about yourself and the way you operate, the easier it should be to adjust to changes.)

Enjoy taking the Self-Discovery Quiz on the next page, but don't be surprised if, like the Donny and Marie Osmond song title says, you're "A Little Bit Country, A Little Bit Rock 'N Roll"!

IF THE SHOE FITS, WEAR IT!

1. I don't like small talk.
   a. That's my shoe!
   b. Small talk is useful and okay with me.
2. I may do fine at parties, but afterward, I need some quiet hours.
   a. Parties? The more the merrier.
   b. That's my shoe!
3. I can't imagine why someone would want to be left alone!
   a. That's my shoe!
   b. Some people need more *space* than others.
4. Internal types are arrogant.
   a. That may or may not be true.
   b. Same as A!
5. I want to be alone.
   a. That's my shoe!
   b. Only for a very short time.
6. It bugs me when my spouse or friend tries to draw me out.
   a. My shoe is the one labeled "misunderstood"!
   b. It doesn't bug me.
7. I'm outnumbered by extroverts, or the external types.
   a. I'm in the majority.
   b. That's my shoe!
8. Lucky me; I usually think before I speak.
   a. I constantly remind myself to do that.
   b. That's my shoe.

9. I would love to ask folks to be quiet. I like you, but enough already!
   a. That's my shoe!
   b. Why would I do that?

SCORING: If six or more of these "shoes" fit you, you're probably a lifelong, practicing, internally-wired individual. And you probably know it already. What you may not know is that in recent years, science has learned a good deal about introverts and how they process information. According to "Caring for Your Introvert," an article in the March 2003 issue of *The Atlantic Monthly*, "It's very difficult for an extrovert to understand an introvert." So if you scored two "shoe fits" or fewer, you may not understand your counterpart well, and it could behoove you to consider the matter. At the least, it may prevent a rush to judgment about a boss or someone with whom you currently have differences.

Eight Ways to Make Use of This Information if You're an Internal

Attitude: Keep Your Focus Positive

Remember: The most important attribute of a successful person is attitude with a positive slant. Here is a list of ways to keep your mind focused on the positive side of every event. Post this list next to your desk, in your car, at home by the mirror and, if necessary, inside your laptop case.

- *Keep your mind fixed on your goals. Take a bow! You may find this easier to do than the externally focused individual. You tend to think before you speak, and that can give you the edge when it comes to considering whether what you're about to say will propel you forward or put you into a stalled position.*

- *Laugh in the face of adversity. Go ahead; laugh aloud. You might enjoy the sound and the release of tension that frequently accompanies the gesture. If you choose to do this in the privacy of your own car, in the stall in the restroom or any other private place, it doesn't matter. The goal is to establish a positive mindset, and you will accomplish the goal whether you're alone or with others.*

- *Get excited by every achievement, no matter how small. You probably tend to be reserved, but go ahead and jump up and down when there's something that warrants it. If you prefer to show excitement in some other way, perhaps a reward such as a midweek trip to the movies, do it your way, but do it!*

- *Never dwell on misfortunes; they are mental depressants. This strategy is self-explanatory. Be aware, however, that if you tend to keep things to yourself, you may add more weight to the misfortune than someone who chats about it with others and therefore receives some positive feedback to help neutralize weighty thoughts.*

- *Associate with people who have a positive outlook. You already know that you must reach out to interact with people if you're to succeed in the workplace. Since that takes more effort than it does for an externally focused person, don't be so riveted by the effort itself that you neglect to be selective.*

- *Treat each experience as another step toward your dreams. Even when you must attend large conventions, mix and mingle in crowds, spend considerable time glad-handing and have little time for self-renewal. Herald the opportunity. It may not be your favorite environment in which to operate, but it's another experience that helps to take you where you want to go.*

- *Commitment, action and self-esteem determine your outcomes. If you believe this, own it! Post this observation where you'll see it often. Your internally focused self need not labor at a disadvantage even if introverts are in the minority in this population.*

- *Consistency is not a luxury; it's a necessity! It may be that even when you repeat all the positive moves you become familiar with, you won't be comfortable with all of them. Recognize these actions as a necessity, and get on with it. Of course, you control your attitude. Put a positive light on whatever you're doing, and even though you don't enjoy the process, you should enjoy the fact that the action is taking you where you wish to go.*

Inner Circle

S E C T I O N   T H R E E

Digging Deeper/Depth and Breadth of the Job

How-to-do-it information was promised earlier in this book and here it is! The following topics are addressed:

1. Appointment Coordination
2. Manager Support
3. Managing Office Technology
4. Meeting Preparation & Coordination
5. Office Communication
6. Office Organization
7. Problem Solving
8. Professional Behavior & Image
9. Professional Development
10. Supporting Multiple Managers
11. Task & Project Management
12. Time Management

It's impractical to discuss any one of these topics without trespassing slightly onto others in the lineup. Nevertheless, each topic is essentially a standalone. So let your priorities guide you. For example, if you'd like immediate information about Office Communication, go directly to Office Communication and obtain what you need. Plan to read all of the chapters at your leisure. Refer to any one of them at any time should you desire a refresher.

COMPETENCY 1

APPOINTMENT COORDINATION

Managing a calendar effectively is a valuable skill. It's critical to the organization and productivity of your office. There are many aspects to appointment scheduling with which every administrative professional should be familiar.

The *inner circle* assistant doesn't just rely upon a calendar when she schedules an appointment for the boss. She relies upon big-picture knowledge.

IMAGINE THAT your boss is just returning from a five-day business trip and will need office time to play catch-up. You'll want to keep her first day back in the office freed up for just that purpose. So remember that just because a calendar date appears empty, that doesn't mean the date is available.

Unless you acknowledge the importance of this distinction, you're likely to treat appointment coordination as a time-management task and miss a ready-made opportunity to shine!

IMAGINE THAT you employ stringent gate-keeping rules prior to meetings that are likely to be demanding. You'll free the boss to concentrate on meeting preparation without distraction. Surely, this kind of pampering isn't frivolous; it enables your boss to be more productive. And you're directly responsible for that result.

First Things First

Ideal assistant/manager teams are those in which the assistant is responsible, with the manager, for scheduling appointments. When that happens, you're likely to be using a mutually agreeable calendar tool for maintaining information. If, however, you and your boss schedule appointments independently from one another, it's likely that the boss has a calendar and you have a calendar. Sometimes, each of you may have more than one calendar. On top of that, different kinds of calendars—pocket calendars, computer calendars or the favorite, desk calendars—may be in use. With all these calendars floating around, how do you make sure appointments aren't missed and changes are made to all pertinent calendars?

It doesn't take a rocket scientist to realize that the first thing to do is make sure you and the executive or executives you support are always looking at the same information.

Reviewing Calendars

If more than one scheduling calendar is in use, take the initiative and ask your boss to show it to you at regular intervals:

How Often	*Purpose*
Every morning	Discuss the day's events with your manager(s). Make any necessary changes, deletions or additions. Contact any appropriate individuals regarding changes.
Weekly	Review events in upcoming weeks. This allows you and your manager time to discuss and prepare agendas and materials and to make necessary changes without waiting until the last minute.
Monthly	Compare your calendar with your manager's as far as three months out. This gives you plenty of time to discuss, coordinate and prepare as much as possible for future events. It suggests when you should and should not plan time off. Coordinating calendars helps the assistant be knowledgeable and sound intelligent when questioned about upcoming events.

On occasion, ask for general feedback with the goal of identifying adjustments that need to be made to increase productivity and reduce stress.

No doubt you can add to the following reminders. Please do!

- *Anticipate the manager's needs. This eliminates last-minute running around and the possibility of necessary materials not being found in time for a meeting.*
- *Prepare for critical time crunches. Will seasonal demands or other predictable time requirements make out-of-the-ordinary arrangements desirable? Should temporary employees be hired? Or should you solicit help from coworkers? It may be as basic as asking a co-*

worker to handle all your incoming calls. You can repay the favor by doing the same for him when he experiences a time crunch. (As they say, "Forewarned is forearmed.")

- *Watch for pertinent mail that arrives just prior to a meeting. Flag it for your boss.*

Post-Meeting Chores

There are three parts to meeting planning: 1) pre-meeting, 2) the meeting and 3) post-meeting. *This last part is frequently over-looked.*

Who makes sure that things get done after the meeting? You can help by questioning your manager when he or she returns from the meeting.

"Is there anything you need to do to fulfill a promise you made at the meeting?" Also, ask if the manager has requested *action items* you need to follow up on or look for in the mail.

TIPS AT A GLANCE

- Learn your manager's appointment preferences.
- Give your manager time between appointments to review mail, return phone calls and work on priority items.
- Do not schedule meetings as soon as your manager returns to the office from lunch.
- Avoid appointments for the first thing Monday morning or the last thing Friday afternoon.
- Allow extra time for travel when scheduling meetings outside the office.
- Allow time in the morning for your manager to get organized.
- Allow time at the end of the day for your manager to wrap up and prepare for the next day.

Then & Now—A Looking-Glass View

Then: Technology had not come onto the scene. Paper calendars were standard, and entries were made on them.

Now: Some bosses are technically competent and use a Palm Pilot and other electronic tools. The *inner circle* assistant has to coordinate all entries so that appointments are kept, productivity isn't compromised and embarrassments are avoided. (For example, "I'm sorry I can't meet with you on Tuesday. I completely forgot about a previous engagement.")

The *inner circle* assistant has electronic access to multiple calendars and can, for example, judge who is available to attend a meeting. She does more analyses than her yesteryear relative. She uses her brain to evaluate the big picture. *What will this involve for my executive? Will he have time to read and respond to e-mails? Will she have time to return phone calls? What's scheduled in two or three weeks? Should I schedule this meeting after other meetings have taken place? Would this benefit my boss?*

COMPETENCY 2

MANAGER SUPPORT

Two to Tango

You and the person you support make up a team, even if it's a small team.

There are three stages in a team relationship.

The *first* is learning to work together. Within that stage, each person tries to understand the other person's work habits, communication style and attitude. It's a getting-to-know-you stage.

The *second* stage revolves around partnership development. That encompasses knowing each other on a deeper level, such as knowing each other's work values, specific likes and dislikes, the scope and depth of each other's jobs, working in concert and seeing differences as assets, rather than liabilities, to the team.

The *third* stage, and probably the most rewarding one, is what I call *synergy*. It's when two people *click* in spite of having different views and opinions. It results in anticipating the next step before your work partner tells you what it is or anticipating the next question he or she is going to ask.

In this chapter, we'll focus on the earliest stages. Stage three is often a by-product, or bonus, that comes from honing the other two stages.

Keep Dancing

In more than 27 years of working with, interviewing and coaching executives and office staff, I have realized that stellar teams *work* at building and maintaining good relationships. They build it step by step and continuously monitor that relationship. There are very few teams who enjoy instant rapport and work in unison.

Whether you work together one month or one year, it's rewarding to create a star team. It makes work more enjoyable, reduces stress and benefits the entire organization.

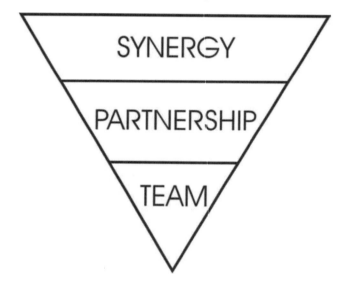

Just as each section of the pyramid expands so does each stage of the team relationship.

IS PERCEPTION REALITY?

Activity: Take a moment to complete the statements below. Provide four to six answers for each one. This brief exercise is intended to help you better identify the role you play.

1. I believe the main functions of an administrative professional are:

   _____

   _____

   _____

   _____

   _____

2. I believe the main functions of a manager are:

   _____

   _____

   _____

   _____

   _____

3. My perceptions of a stellar manager/administrative team are:

   _____

   _____

   _____

   _____

   _____

It's widely accepted that if you perceive you should work independently, make decisions and be a part of the management team, that's what you'll do. If you believe your job is to take specific directions, do only what you are told and not stretch into new territory, that is what you will do. This seems simple enough but…

What If…

…you perceive yourself as being assertive but not everyone agrees? You may, for example, be demure when dealing with a group of upper management people. Why? Are you intimidated? Do you know that some of your skills are not finely honed? If the people you work with and for don't see you the way you see yourself, what then? The *inner circle* assistant realizes that the way others assess her is their reality. In order to be most effective, the *inner circle* assistant needs them to have faith in her and her capabilities.

An Effectiveness Assessment

This activity is designed to expand the lines of communication and set developmental goals. It's interesting to see whether you and the manager you support would score the following in the same way. (Feel free to make a copy of the grid for your boss to use. He or she may be happy to cooperate. You won't know if you don't ask.)

Activity: Review each item on the grid and place an X under the appropriate number (each represents a percentage) or N/A if not applicable.

Effectiveness Grid

	N/A	20	40	60	80	100
Organize and coordinate projects						
Coordinate accomplishment of manager's priority tasks						
Manage multiple projects						
Recommend improved systems and procedures						
Conduct meetings for support staff						
Represent manager(s) in business meetings						
Delegate and explain tasks to other support staff						
Negotiate purchases or contracts						
Compare supplier costs and benefits						
Attend professional development seminars						
Set up systems to organize work						
Draft and edit correspondence						
Set goals and create plans						
Gather background information and materials for meetings						
Promote image of the office						
Act as a liaison for manager(s) to key people						
Resolve conflicts in the office						
Act as first-contact customer service representative						
Create presentations						
Suggest possible solutions to problems						

	N/A	20	40	60	80	100
Advise manager(s) concerning ethical factors						
Counsel administrative staff about performance						
Prepare materials for meetings						
Set up meeting room						
Write courtesy notes and cards						
Maintain a clean, attractive office						
Make calls on behalf of manager(s)						
Receive, greet and introduce visitors						
Arrange lunches and refreshments for meetings						
Operate and troubleshoot office machines						
Write instructions and procedures						
Schedule appointments, meetings and other activities						
Track completion of follow-up tasks						
Take and prepare minutes for meetings						
Manage budget, bills and invoices						
Answer questions about the organization						
Discuss priorities and problems with manager(s)						
Make travel arrangements for manager(s)						
Analyze trends in office technology						

*The blank spaces above are provided to add your own job-specific responsibilities.

Scoring: If you and your manager participated in the Effectiveness Assessment, this next step is a natural: Fill in and sign the Improvement Agreement. Meet again in 30 days to discuss your progress.

IMPROVEMENT AGREEMENT

The following areas were scored as 60 or less:

1. _____
2. _____
3. _____
4. _____
5. _____

My plans for improvement are as follows:

1. _____
2. _____
3. _____
4. _____
5. _____

Date _____
Employee's
Signature _____

Date _____
Manager's
Signature _____

An improvement plan puts you on the road to success!

Talk to Me

Because of the multiple daily activities in the office, it's important for work partners to establish scheduled time to meet without interruption. The best time to do this is in the morning. If you wait until the end of the day, it may never happen, as things tend to build as the day progresses. Make it known to others in the department or immediate area that, barring emergencies, this is uninterruptible time.

If you're wondering what to discuss at these meetings, here are a few ideas:

Daily Calendars

Sometimes schedules change, meetings do not get entered on calendars or wrong times get entered. It's always best to review the day's events together. This is also the time to discuss meetings your manager wants to add for the day or upcoming week.

Telephone Messages

Discuss messages that need immediate attention or response. You can return calls if you have responses from your manager or the required information.

Review Mail

Your manager may want to respond verbally to correspondence or tell you how to respond.

Visitors

Discuss any events that outside visitors will be attending. Get the detailed information you need to help you prepare for such events.

Department Issues

This is a good time to discuss departmental problems that need your manager's attention.

Status Updates

Provide your manager with updates on projects, meetings, items you are working on and any other pertinent information.

Upcoming Travel

Find out about upcoming trips so you can anticipate schedules and prepare travel materials.

Follow-Up Items

Bring to your manager's attention information requested from staff that you have not yet received. Let your manager know whose work you have received.

Training

Tell your manager about upcoming seminars and workshops you would like to attend and why. Be prepared to show your manager information about the workshop, the objectives of the program, how the topics tie in with your job responsibilities and the benefits of attending. If you recently attended a seminar or training session, provide a short evaluation. Explain how you intend to carry out the strategies and methods you discovered, and ask for your manager's cooperation if needed.

Special Projects

Find out what special projects your manager is working on or has coming up in the next few weeks. Is there any research that needs to be done? Will information for the project be coming from others inside or outside the company? Can you start assembling information? Are graphs or charts required? How many are needed? (And so forth.)

It might seem like these meetings would take a tremendous amount of time, but they don't if you meet on a regular basis, because things don't have a chance to build up.

Maximize the Value of Your Together Time

1. Prepare. Bring prioritized notes to the meeting.
2. Don't allow others to interrupt you unless absolutely necessary.
3. Stay focused on the topics being discussed.
4. Bring closure or identify the next step to everything you discuss.
5. Clarify and confirm who is taking on which responsibility.
6. Give each other quick, clear, status updates on previously discussed projects.

Feedback Time

You may or may not want to confine feedback to these early-morning meetings. It may be better to speak out as soon as you're confronted with an issue. You'll be the judge of that, but when you offer feedback, you're well advised to:

- *Confront the problem head on and stay focused.*
- *If possible, prepare notes and refer to them as you speak. Don't rush.*
- *Be specific. Provide examples (e.g., "The quality of work suffers.").*
- *If time permits, practice what you're going to say.*
- *Control your body language and facial expressions. Be professional.*
- *Listen to your manager's version. Try to be understanding.*
- *Even if you don't get your manager to change this behavior, thank her for taking time to meet with you. You may be surprised and see some changes later.*

In reading the following exchange, imagine that you are Brenda.

Brenda: I wanted to talk to you about some of the projects we are currently working on. I'm unclear about your expectations. As we have learned over the past few weeks, when I'm unclear, it creates rework for both of us. In order for us to become more productive and to be credible, I would like to offer a couple of suggestions.

Ms. Executive: Tell me more.

Brenda: I'd like to suggest that we schedule ongoing meetings with each other to encourage sharing of information and expectations. I believe this will make us more effective and productive in completing projects in a timely manner and help us to understand each other's styles as we partner.

Ms. Executive: I am glad you brought this to my attention. I felt your frustration and recognized that it would be beneficial for us to better understand how we can improve our lines of communication. What do you suggest?

Brenda: I would like to start by setting up morning meetings for the two of us, three times per week. This will help me to communicate your schedule and better prepare you for upcoming appointments. Do you have any other suggestions?

Ms. Executive: That sounds great. Let's give it a try.

Brenda: Thank you for taking the time to meet with me.

What Makes Your Manager Tick?

As you strive to become an *inner circle* assistant or maintain your position as an *inner circle* assistant, you focus heavily on who you are, what you want, what you can do and so forth. Take a moment to analyze your boss. Who is the boss? What does the boss want? The more you understand this individual, the better able you are to communicate with the boss and to achieve goals.

The following excerpt is from *Mind of a Manager, Soul of a Leader* by Craig R. Hickman.

"The words 'manager' and 'leader' are metaphors representing two opposite ends of a continuum. 'Manager' tends to signify the more analytical, structured, controlled, deliberate, and orderly end of the continuum, while 'leader' tends to occupy the more experimental, visionary, flexible, uncontrolled, and creative end. Given these fairly universal metaphors of contrasting organizational behavior, I like to think of the prototypical manager as the person who brings the thoughts of the mind to bear on daily organization problems in contrast; the leader brings the feelings of the soul to bear on those same problems. Certainly, managers and leaders both have minds and souls, but they each tend to emphasize one over the other as they function in organizations. The mind represents the analytical, calculating, structuring, and ordering side of tasks and organizations. The soul, on the other hand, represents the visionary, passionate, creative, and flexible side."

Leader Orientation	Manager Orientation
Visionary	Task-oriented
Challenges employees to go out of their comfort zones	Keeps people in their comfort zones
Revolutionizes	Refines present things
Doesn't like stagnation	Strives to maintain the status quo
Optimistic	Pessimistic
Creates change	Values stability in the face of change
Creates a new culture	Preserves current culture
Focuses on opportunity	Sees danger
Provides inspiration, encouragement	Gives instruction
Empowers employees	Tends to be controlling
Thrives on crisis	Strives for stability
Has vision for overall purpose	Limits imagination and creativity
Favors unstructured approach	Prefers structured approach

You may know just from reading these characteristics which orientation best describes the person to whom you report. This person might also display some characteristics of both. Tuck this quick analysis into the back pocket of your thoughts and use it to your advantage.

IMAGINE THAT your boss strives to maintain the status quo. (If he were a leader type, he would not like stagnation.) When you make an offer, you want it to be an offer he or she won't refuse. Since you recognize that your boss strives to maintain the status quo, you'll be careful not to suggest anything too grand. For example, if you want to alter the desk placements and use of space on the department floor, you can point to reasons why this would benefit your boss. "Bob, why don't we rearrange the desks around your office cubicle? It would only take maintenance staff a short time to do this, and you would probably notice that your office is quieter. You'll get work done without so many distractions. The people using the desks will benefit, too. They'll have quicker access to supplies they need from the supply room. This should boost efficiency."

At a later date, you may go back to Bob and suggest that the rest of the desks be rearranged, too.

When you use this strategy, *you exhibit a leader orientation.* You're a visionary! Of course, you have a little help because you have some understanding of what makes your boss tick!

A Competitive Edge

Your manager needs to be in the forefront whether he or she owns a business or is a sales representative within a firm. You continue building your partnership and reaching synergy by helping your manager maintain a competitive edge in his professional actions, behaviors and words. Partners want to make each other look good to others inside and outside the organization. It's something you both work at consistently. When your manager looks good to the outside world and stands out in the organization, so do you. When you are professional in all aspects of your job, your manager appears in a positive light to others within the organization.

Know Your Industry

- *Know your competition. Learn how competing firms differ from your company and if they offer the same products or services.*

- *Know as much about your company as possible. You should be able to answer questions about products and services or at least know the appropriate person for referrals.*
- *Stay current on news and changes within your industry. You can do this by reading newspapers, magazines and trade publications.*
- *Clip articles that may be of interest to your boss.*
- *Be alert to the media. If you hear or see something relevant to your company, write down the station, time and program, and pass it on to your manager.*

Be a Professional Agent of Your Company

- *Develop a pleasant telephone manner.*
- *Learn how to handle angry clients or customers tactfully.*
- *Create good feelings with everyone.*
- *Express a friendly attitude in all business dealings.*
- *Do not bring your bad moods to the office.*
- *Resist the temptation to gossip or complain.*
- *Learn to discuss specific problems with your manager or other appropriate management personnel.*
- *Be a source of events and news.*
- *Listen patiently.*
- *Be dependable.*

Be Prepared to Turn Failure into Success

The *inner circle* assistant brings a healthy attitude to the job. Even when faced with failure, the *inner circle* assistant responds like a star!

Our success-oriented society often makes it difficult for those who fail to adjust. This negative attitude often forces people to take job-related failures personally, even if they had little to do with the actual events.

When failure occurs: Many people go through a mourning process similar to that for the death of a loved one:

1. Denial
2. Bargaining
3. Anger
4. Depression
5. Acceptance

While no one embraces failure, some people take it harder than others, blaming themselves entirely for their lack of foresight. Embarrassed to face their colleagues, unable to confide in their friends or family, they are isolated in their own grief.

Bounce back after failure:

1. Acknowledge the failure. When this first, vital step isn't taken, an atmosphere of fear is created. Instead, face your failure and see that it is an opportunity to learn and grow.
2. Ask for help in preventing future failures. If the guilty party doesn't request help, it may lead this person to say, "I'll just be more careful next time. I won't take such a big risk again." And that sort of thinking leads to stagnation and a loss of creativity and growth for both individuals and organizations.
3. Failure can be an opportunity to reflect, rethink values and interests and then make positive changes. People are often better off after they've failed, because if it hadn't been for their missteps, they might still be in the same corporate rut.

REMEMBER: The beginning of a year provides a great opportunity to set new goals and make a commitment to improve areas of your professional life. The first entry you might want to make on a new calendar is this one: "It's time to set new goals. It's time to improve areas of my professional life. It's time to get specific!"

One key area to look at is your relationship with your immediate manager or supervisor. Is it where you want it to be? If not, what can you do about it? If it is where you want it, how can you take it to the next level? Are you performing the tasks you think you should? Are you doing things you think you shouldn't have to do? Are you guessing or do you ask, "Did I handle this to your liking?" or "What did you think of the monthly report I put together?" or "What do you think I can do to improve this report?" (These are just a few questions you should ask yourself when viewing this very important relationship.)

By the way, I know what it's like to be on both sides of the desk. I've been a business owner since 1990, and I can honestly say that I have a different perspective of management than I did when I was an employee. Try to understand what it is like to be in your manager's shoes — the tough decisions she has to make, the people problems, the stress from her boss or the company. Likewise, try to help your manager see what it's like to be in your shoes.

Accepting the Gift

As you request and receive feedback from coworkers and managers, you want to develop the skill of accepting feedback. While some people aren't the best at offering constructive criticism, you can still benefit from it. Here are some techniques to help you.

- *Try to schedule face-to-face meetings with your manager. Some managers dislike providing critical feedback one on one. So they end up writing criticisms on paper or e-mail. This just raises tensions. If your manager operates this way, let him or her know that you prefer to discuss these things face to face.*

- *If you're the victim of public humiliation, calmly take the person who is criticizing you aside. Tell her that you would like to know how you can improve but would rather keep such discussions between the two of you.*
- *Don't become defensive, argumentative or angry. Instead, ask how you can specifically do things differently. And take notes.*
- *If you disagree with the feedback, simply change the perceptions. Criticism allows you to know how you are being perceived. So if the perception is wrong, don't get angry; change it.*
- *Act on the information. Let your supervisor know about your attempts to improve. This way you can demonstrate that you're sincere about improving your work.*

Think Before You React

It's almost instinctive to yell back or to be offended at someone who is yelling at us, be it a coworker or a boss. But yelling back or arguing accomplishes little. It can destroy a business relationship and certainly dim your professional image.

Then & Now — A Looking-Glass View

Then: Assistants didn't manage the business; they just did the task. They didn't have power. Even good partnerships didn't rise to the level of *synergy* that is possible today.

Now: The *inner circle* assistant sits down to discuss the department's projects and is involved in decision making. The *inner circle* assistant understands the scope of the business and therefore appreciates the value attached to an action. For example, if today's assistant says, "I know what my boss does. She's a speaker," she's not identifying the scope. She would be more likely to say, "My boss trains *inner circle* assistants so they prosper and the companies that employ them prosper, too. Here's how..." The fact that the boss is a speaker is only incidental to the big picture. Today's *inner circle* assistant knows this. This individual also initiates actions, actually helps to run the business.

COMPETENCY 3

Managing Office Technology

Office technology proliferates, and if we don't manage it, it will probably manage us. This chapter moves quickly, pausing here and there to offer you valuable information. It's challenging to be up to the minute in this venue, but *try we must*. One way to accomplish the goal is to be inquisitive, willing to learn and keeping an open mind. When you do, just about anything is possible!

Electronic Mail

E-mail is an excellent tool for communicating general, non-urgent corporate communications, such as the minutes of meetings, news releases, reports and memos. And even though many people enjoy real-time e-mail delivery, others don't have this service. You can't assume that someone will see your message as soon as you send it.

Brainstorming sessions or philosophical debates waged over e-mail are frustrating. Exciting observations can only move at the speed of typing fingers; a more satisfying experience is possible by using the telephone if a face-to-face session isn't possible. Experts offer these observations:

- *Make sure important issues are talked about, not typed about.*
- *Avoid the urgent e-mail message for time-critical information.*
- *The auto-reply feature of your e-mail software can help you by automatically sending a response to each incoming message announcing that you are out of the office.*

- *Be assertive. Notify message senders when you want to be taken off their distribution lists.*
- *Take time to master all of your e-mail software's features.*

E-mail Tips

These tips are provided by John Bowie, a Colorado-based information engineering executive and consultant.

- *Check e-mail messages at set times of the day to not interrupt your work load every time a message board flashes.*
- *Know your company's e-mail culture. What's permitted? What's not?*
- *Carefully choose those to whom you send information.*
- *Some people say the subject line is the most important part of any e-mail message. Be succinct but informative. This will help recipients prioritize their e-mail and know which messages to open first.*
- *Remember to present your best work. E-mail reflects the individual sending it. Be sure that e-mail messages are properly formatted.*
- *Get to the point! E-mail makes it easy to efficiently communicate important information, especially when you craft messages using bullets and short paragraphs.*
- *E-mail is public information. When you're crafting a message, you should consider not only who is going to read it today but who might read it a year from now.*
- *Every business e-mail user should be aware of "flames," which are written personal insults or extreme expressions of opinion; used too often, they can burn out your career.*

Cellular Telephones

Cellular telephones are a remarkable convenience since theoretically you're able to be in touch at all times. They've created a way to make downtime more productive. At the same time, by using a cellular telephone improperly, you can become one of the growing number of rude "techno blunderers"!

- *Cellular telephone technology is good but not perfect, so always let someone know if you're calling from your car or cellular telephone in case you're suddenly cut off.*
- *Never discuss sensitive or confidential information on your cellular telephone. Eavesdropping technology is also advanced.*
- *When using your telephone in the car, be careful! Pull over to the side of the road or into a parking lot. If you must use your telephone while in transit, don't dial while you're driving. You might consider installing a speakerphone or using a hands-free device.*
- *Don't use your telephone in crowded areas. Be aware that you may be disturbing others. And it's never an exercise in good manners to broadcast your conversations.*

Working Together Although We're Apart

The 21st century challenges us to work and interact differently. With the changes in office design, technology advancements, flex time, employees working from homes and the virtual office, we have to learn to work together from a distance. E-mail, cell phones and other latter-day technologies help with that challenge, especially if used as advised.

There's more:

- *Set up mini-sessions where you can meet face to face.*
- *Write a time map and responsibility sheet.*
- *Responsibilities must be clear, detailed and specific.*
- *Give each other regular status updates.*
- *Take responsibility for your part of the assignment.*

And don't forget to rely upon old-fashioned skill, attitude, teamwork and success strategies to help you achieve goals.

Maximize the Value of Time Spent Together

Because many administrative office professionals work with managers who travel extensively, are out of the office frequently or are just tech savvy and use that technology while in the office, it's imperative to make the most of together time.

Managers and assistants must work in harmony and as a team to accomplish tasks, reach corporate goals and be truly productive. Lines of communication must be open and in excellent working order.

IMAGINE THAT you can identify barriers to success when you're meeting with your manager, teammate or other people you support. What things hinder you from having productive together time? If you can't crystallize the reasons and put them into words, ask your manager, teammate or other people you support in this long-distance arrangement to answer the question. Barriers can't be rectified until they're identified!

_____

_____

_____

_____

_____

_____

_____

_____

Techno Etiquette

Barbara Pachter, president of Pachter & Associates, says that whether you realize it or not, people often judge the competence and courtesy of a business operation by the way someone answers a telephone or the quality of the voice mail greeting.

Today, telephone etiquette is much more complex than simply answering with a "smile in your voice." Today, there is new voice mail, car and cellular telephone technology. "We haven't learned the proper rules regarding advanced telephone etiquette in large part because these techno-advances literally exploded on the scene. We had no choice but to hit the ground running."

Interestingly, business professionals identify telephone skills as one of the most abused skills. Your oral skills say a lot about you and your company. You want to be certain you send the best message possible to internal and external customers.

Think about the phone calls you made in the last two months. How often has the person answering the phone:

	OFTEN	SOME- TIMES	NEVER
Left you on hold for more than 30 seconds?			
Failed to identify the company's name?			
Reflected an unfriendly tone?			
Neglected to say "please" or "thank you"?			
Acted as though you were interrupting them?			
Not sensed the urgency of your call?			
Written the wrong phone number or misspelled your name or your company name?			
Not ended the conversation on a pleasant note?			

If some of these memories make you shudder, think of them as lessons for what not to do.

Voice mail should be used to:

- *Convey information quickly.*
- *Reach someone you may not normally have access to.*
- *Keep communications more personal than e-mail or fax.*

It shouldn't be used to:

- *Introduce yourself to someone.*
- *Offer condolences.*
- *Convey confidential or critical information.*

- *Negotiate.*
- *Criticize someone.*

Recording Winning Messages

- *Identify yourself and your department.*
- *Be professional. Don't leave cutesy messages at the office.*
- *Update your messages regularly.*
- *Before recording your message, practice.*

Make sure you answer these questions:
- *Where are you?*
- *When will you return?*
- *When can you return phone calls?*
- *How can you be reached in an emergency?*
- *Who else can help in your absence?*

Employ a pleasant tone and positive attitude:
- *Try not to use a monotone.*
- *Be positive and upbeat.*
- *Make the caller feel that you care.*
- *Smile!*

When it's time to leave a message for someone else, be sure to include the following:
- *Your name, company name and/or department name (internal calls).*
- *Date and time of your call.*
- *The reason for your call.*
- *When you will be in your office and how you can be reached.*
- *Speak clearly, distinctly and slowly.*
- *Leave your telephone number. Don't assume the person has memorized your number or is listening to messages with a Rolodex handy.*

Worthy of note:

You can cut the length of phone calls about 40 percent by creating a mini-agenda for each call you make. Simply jot down key words for all the points you want to address during a call. Studies show that planned-out business calls last an average of seven minutes, while unplanned calls average 12 minutes. (Source: *Organize Your Life & Get Rid of Clutter* by Ab Jackson.)

Plan to gather any papers, notes or files before making the call. Ask for the name of the person who answers the phone and make a note of it. Give your name, company name and the name of the person you wish to speak to. Express a positive, optimistic tone. Project warm and sincere feelings. Vary your pitch. Use a medium rate of speed and speak clearly. Promptly return all calls, unless you don't wish to respond (e.g., A salesman may be attempting to solicit business. You're not bound to respond to this call.)

On a Personal Note, Get Moving

Our bodies are designed to move, not stay in one position all day. So if you spend your workday pounding on computer keys and making good use of other techno-wonders, it's important to give your body a break. Here are some tips to help you move from your desk throughout the day.

1. Build in short tasks throughout the day that force you to walk away from the desk every 20 to 30 minutes. Get printouts, do some filing, confer with a coworker. Ideally, the tasks should involve walking, standing and stretching.

2. Frequent, short breaks are better than fewer, longer breaks. But when lunchtime rolls around, try to get in at least a quick walk around the block.

3. When you take breaks, try to stretch the muscles and joints that were in one position for an extended period of time. And relax those that were active.

4. Use a timer or software to remind you to take a break.

5. Periodically alter your sitting position, and always keep your hands and wrists warm.

6. Try standing while you work on the computer.

Risk-Free E-mail

"One of the easiest and most effective ways for employers to reduce electronic risk is simply to require that employees use appropriate, businesslike language in all electronic communications," says Nancy Flynn, author of *The ePolicy Handbook*.

Here are some of the guidelines she recommends in composing business e-mail:

- **Use a conversational tone.** *Flynn says to imagine you are attending a dinner party with colleagues, supervisors and customers. Use the same language and tone in an e-mail that you would use at that kind of event.*
- **Don't be overly rigid with grammar use.** *In business, those rules have changed. Feel free to use contractions, to end sentences with prepositions and to use pronouns like "I," "we" and "you." If grammar is too stiff, readers won't know what the message is about.*
- **No sexist language.** *This isn't just harassing or discriminatory jokes and comments but also the overuse of masculine pronouns. Given the increasing number of women in the work force, it's important for electronic writers to avoid language that could rankle clients or colleagues.*

- *Don't incorporate jokes into electronic business writing. Because e-mail is impersonal and lacks inflection or body language, your joke is likely to fall flat or to be misconstrued.*
- *Limit the use of abbreviations and use only legitimate and recognizable ones, not your own personal shorthand. An excess of abbreviations can be annoying and confusing for the reader.*
- *Don't try to warm up business writing with "smileys" (commonly known as emoticons) — smiles and similar facial expressions made with keyboard characters). They are the equivalent of e-mail slang and have no place in business communications.*

Writing E-mail That Get Results

If you find that it takes days to get a reply to your e-mail — if you even get one at all — you probably need to re-evaluate how you're using the technology. Here are eight tips on writing e-mails that get better and faster results:

Keep it as short as possible. If you want your entire message to be read, write it to fit on one screen, no more than 25 lines. Write short paragraphs with spaces in between. Save longer letters and memos for fax and snail mail.

Don't beat around the bush. If you want a person to do something, let him know in the second sentence of your message what that is. Then close the note by restating what you're asking for and any deadlines.

Don't send mystery messages. Never send an e-mail that doesn't have a short, descriptive subject line. Put action into it; for example, "Need to reschedule meeting."

Number your points. If you're reiterating points made in a meeting or listing tasks that need to be acted on, bullet or number the points.

Don't skimp on punctuation. Correct grammar encourages people to take your message seriously.

Be wary about sending attachments. Unless you're sure the recipient wants or needs the documents, don't send any with your e-mail message. And if you do have to send several documents, send them separately with an appropriate, descriptive subject line. It saves the recipient from having to retrieve the attachment as part of a long list of other documents.

Check your date and time. Double-check the time and date on your computer and/or your company's e-mail server. If it's mis-dated or mistimed, your e-mail could end up in the wrong place in your recipient's inbox.

Include a signature. Most e-mail programs provide an automatic signature file that attaches your name and contact information at the bottom of every e-mail message. Use it.

Then & Now — A Looking-Glass View

Then: Office technology consisted of a telephone, copy machine, a facsimile machine and not much else. Computers arrived on the scene with one or two software programs.

Now: So many things are techno-driven. For one, some employees routinely work away from the office. Technology has made this feasible. They connect with one another and with their colleagues at the office using cell phones, setting up conference calls and relying heavily on voice messaging equipment.

The *inner circle* assistant has got to truly be computer literate. She or he is probably skilled with PowerPoint and Excel programs. Spreadsheets are a latter-day arrival. Bar graphs and charts that can be generated electronically are put to use in simple office reports. This kind of sophistication was unheard of back in the old days.

I wrote about this matter in detail in my 2003 book *Real-World Communication Strategies That Work.*

COMPETENCY 4

Meeting Preparation & Coordination

UPSURGE IN MEETINGS

You probably spend a lot of time scheduling, changing, preparing for and attending meetings. Maybe you thought that with all the new technology available, the number of meetings held would decrease. Actually, there is an upsurge in meetings. The average number of meetings jumped from seven to about 10 per week, say national surveys. According to the 3M Meeting Network, business professionals spend from 25 percent to 60 percent of their time in meetings. It's also reported that as much as 50 percent of that time is unproductive and that as much as 25 percent of meeting time covers irrelevant issues.

According to *USA Today*, the upsurge is being driven by several workplace shifts:

- *Rise in teams and requisite team meetings.*
- *Technology such as videoconferencing allows meetings despite distance barriers.*
- *Job cuts trimming middle management require more communication between workers because of fewer go-betweens.*

Meetings have a bad reputation as being ineffective and a waste of time. They don't have to be. They are essential to an organization's success. If you and your colleagues follow these guidelines, you can meet with success!

Elements of an Effective Meeting

Experts agree that one reason many meetings are such a waste is because no one really prepares for them. In addition, some meetings aren't necessary. As an administrative professional, maybe you can't control what meetings get scheduled and by whom, but you can assist in the preparation, whether or not you are an attendee. Here are some meeting musts from *USA Today* for you or your manager(s).

- *Have a reason for the meeting. Identify the objective for your meeting.*
- *Distribute an agenda to participants before the meeting.*
- *Give participants at least one day's notification.*
- *Participants should know what is expected of them.*
- *Limit attendance and designate a leader.*
- *Set time limits for the meeting and each topic to be covered.*
- *Distribute materials in advance if at all possible.*
- *Let participants know about outcomes.*

Facilitating Successful Meetings

Administrative professionals are increasingly being asked to attend meetings and facilitate meetings. Before you can do either like an *inner circle* achiever, you need to know something about the anatomy of a productive meeting.

Elements of a Productive Meeting

- *Stated objective.*
- *Input from attendees.*
- *Delegation of tasks.*
- *Positive outcomes.*
- *Attendees actively listen.*
- *Note taking where appropriate.*

- *Result in specific actions to be taken.*
- *Everyone shares ideas while staying on track.*
- *Informative materials and persuasive visual aids.*
- *Rigorous debate and brainstorming while respecting each other's opinion.*

Your Responsibilities as Facilitator (in no particular order of priority)

Pre-Meeting	The Meeting	Post Meeting
Set agenda.	Take the lead.	Send recap of meeting or minutes.
Mail agenda with estimated time frames to attendees.	Show energy.	Confirm tasks assigned to attendees and deadline dates.
Write your objectives and expected outcomes.	Stay focused. Don't let attendees distract you.	Mail any thank-you notes.
Make notes of items to cover.	Check your watch from time to time. Are you on track?	Transfer action items to follow-up lists, calendars and to-do folders.
Jot notes regarding any private questions you have for attendees.	Keep attendees on track. Don't let them go off on tangents.	Update your calendar with future meeting dates.
Start a "Take to Meeting" pile or stack.	Post a list of topics to be covered. Have an attendee check them off as completed.	Put files away that you took to the meeting.
Coordinate or delegate all logistics.	Ask questions of attendees to clarify what you think you heard.	Send necessary information to non-attendees or tell alternate's team leader.

Do your homework. Research topics.	Have attendance roster ready, if required.	Get feedback from attendees.
Designate someone for minutes.	Be on time!	Keep attendees informed of the status of projects discussed in meeting.
Prepare charts and handouts.	Pull files or pertinent information.	Clean conference room and return all equipment.
Check on supplies and visual aids.	Check out meeting room and equipment prior to meeting.	Conduct a meeting survey.
Are lunch and/or refreshments to be served?		Make note of personal lessons learned.
Send directions and other logistical information to attendees outside the organization.		
Confirm meeting in writing or by e-mail.		

Keep Attendees on Track

As a trainer conducting full-day workshops regularly, I am frequently asked how I keep attendees motivated and focused. There are several techniques I use, but here are a few ideas you can definitely enforce when running a meeting:

1. Have a written, time-planned agenda. Once you are in the meeting, frequently check your actual time schedule against your planned schedule. If you get behind, try to figure out what's slowing you down. Is one attendee dominating the conversation? Is someone in the

meeting going off on a tangent and the group with him or her? If so, you need to take control of the conversation and keep everyone moving forward.

IMAGINE WHAT would happen if you armed one attendee with a stopwatch and a whistle and a water gun. One rather sedate executive got so disgusted with meetings that ran overtime, she directed someone to time each spokesperson and blow the whistle at the end of the allotted time. If the speaker didn't STOP, well, you guessed it. The water gun was squirted into the air and got everyone's attention. Things stopped.

2. Have an agenda posted in the room for everyone to see. This can be in addition to individual copies of agendas for each attendee. Check off each item as it is covered. Have an attendee monitor the time and check off accomplishments.

3. Do your best to stay focused. Stay on one topic or problem until you have exhausted it or determined that it will either be finished at another meeting or further discussed after your meeting.

IMAGINE THAT a large and rather ugly piece of pottery sitting on the table in front of you. One *inner circle* assistant had an amazing array of these objects. She loved to attend flea markets and would purchase any ugly item that she could get for $3 to $5. When she looked at it during meetings, it reminded her to focus. She announced to all who were in attendance, "This pottery is a show stopper. It's difficult to permit it to blend into the scenery. Let it be a reminder to us all that our topic can't be allowed to blend into the scenery either. Keep our topic, whatever it is, front and center!" Will this work in your environment? It may seem less than professional to pull a stunt like this, but if it brings desired results, you may agree that it's worth a try.

4. Keep attendees involved through questions and discussion so they don't have time to stray. Ask for their input.

5. Feel comfortable saying, "It seems we've strayed from the subject. We were talking about..."

Follow-Up:

There is a great deal to be learned about each meeting stage. Gather and read materials to continue your professional growth on this important subject.

Help Your Manager Prepare to Attend a Meeting

Now go stand in the corner and look at this whole process from a different direction. You may see that you still have a role to play to ensure that a meeting is more productive. When I introduced this section, I wrote that some topics trespass on others. This is one place it's worth repeating information that appears elsewhere:

- *Anticipate the manager's needs. Does he need the latest warehouse inventory report or new equipment cost comparisons from the purchasing department to back up his assertions? And what materials might be needed for the various meetings? Will she rely upon handouts or use a PowerPoint program or do both? Will he want you to e-mail pertinent information to attendees prior to the meeting so they're prepared to make decisions? Not only will this kind of advanced planning eliminate a potential last-minute scramble to obtain data, it allows time to make contingency plans if data are unavailable.*

- *Anticipate and prepare for critical time crunches. When you know a major meeting is coming up, you can arrange your tasks and projects around anticipated deadlines. Protect your boss from frivolous dis-*

tractions and you'll deliver her to the meeting in good shape to perform.

- *Look for items in the mail pertinent to the upcoming meetings or meetings that have taken place. Highlight those items and bring them to your manager's attention, or place them in a file related to the meeting. He will arrive with up-to-the-minute information at his disposal. This is a time saver and can be expected to favorably impact the bottom line.*

- *The post-meeting is often overlooked. Many times in meetings, attendees are given action items. But what happens after the meeting? Who makes sure they get done? You can help by questioning your manager when he returns from the meeting. Ask if he has requested action items that you need to follow up on or look for in the mail. In this way, the glow of triumph that prevails when a good meeting takes place won't become a fleeting memory. You will see to it that no one drops the ball!*

Then & Now — A Looking-Glass View

Then: The support person took orders and carried them out. She would be a note taker and not a contributor. If she was resourceful, she may have maintained to-do lists so that her tasks were clear and not forgotten in the time between meetings.

Now: The *inner circle* assistant takes some ownership. If, for example, the manager she supports is hosting the meeting, she may have to remind him, "You know, our meeting is less than two weeks away. Can I help sketch out the agenda? Do you want me to prepare a rough draft?" She will design and use forms (e.g., attendance rosters) to get various jobs done. When larger meetings are planned, she will find and use software programs that help plot the meeting and actions needed to ensure success. She often sits in on meetings and participates. It's not surprising for her to contribute ideas. At staff and department meetings, she may be asked to stand and give a ten-minute presentation to inform attendees about what's going on. She may host a meeting for other assistants. Then, she runs the whole show. Today's *inner circle* assistant is expected to make a difference at every stage of the meeting: planning, in progress and follow-up. She is important, and she and her boss know it.

COMPETENCY 5

Office Communication

Communication is the art of exchanging information. In this chapter, we'll explore communication under various circumstances that prevail in office and workplace settings. *It's not your mama's brand of communication*. The end goal here is to generate profits for the company and to keep on keeping on. The *inner circle* assistant and aspiring *inner circle* assistant are well advised to dash through this potpourri of reminders, tips and observations from time to time, since perfecting the art of communication requires constant care and feeding!

Communication Crisis: Building Rapport

Communication crisis, for purposes of this book, is defined as a crisis or conflict occurring between two or more people. The crisis centers around communication problems, such as not listening, not giving enough information or not clearly stating expectations. However, a closer look shows it has more to do with:

- *Personal opinions*
- *Prejudices*
- *Personal goals*
- *Power (One person wants or has power over the other person.)*
- *"I want to win" and "You have to lose" mentality*
- *Hurt feelings (that aren't expressed)*
- *Past events (Your previous interactions and outcome with this person or group of people.)*

- *Stubbornness*
- *Timing (This is just not a good time for the other person for personal or professional reasons.)*

Catalysts and Cures for Communication Crises

No Closure

You or the other person jumps from topic to topic. You never come to closure or complete a topic. Take the lead in staying on the topic at hand by saying, "Let's get back to..." or "You were saying..."

IMAGINE THAT a junior manager asks for information about preparing a year-end report. You spend time assembling all necessary information for her and send it in an e-mail attachment. She fires back that what she really needs is statistics you have on hand regarding absenteeism charts. You check to see if she has clearance to see these reports, and then you supply them. She meets you in the hallway and asks for yet a third item. Days later, you're seated at a meeting table with other people and she berates you. "Why the silence? I need you to review the year-end report. And I'm waiting for end-of-month absenteeism statistics." Essentially, she is switching gears—not finishing one thing and moving ahead to another. Moreover, she makes it appear that you didn't respond to her requests. Everyone else around that table will tell you this person is difficult to deal with. She's disorganized, to say the least. In the future, you don't acquiesce to her latest request until you have closure on the one that preceded it. And you get it in writing.

No Personal Interest

You show no interest in the other person as a person. Personal attention helps maintain good relationships. You don't have to get personal, but showing an interest in someone's opinion or position within the company gives a sense of personal attention that can strengthen communication.

False Assumptions

A sender of information often assumes that the receiver knows the details or intricacies of the topic and therefore leaves gaps in his or her messages. It's important to provide details and/or ask for details.

Not Walking the Walk or Following Through

You or the other person does not follow through on what is said. Or someone changes the agreed-upon event midstream without letting the other person know. These types of people tend to drag down those of us who are trying to accomplish something in a given time frame. Encourage that person to make a firm decision and be supportive.

Lack of Attention

One of the parties is not giving his or her full attention to the other person. First, listen! Take in everything the other person is communicating verbally and nonverbally. Ask questions to check for understanding. Don't evaluate until after you have absorbed.

Quiet-Mouthed

For various reasons, ranging from not feeling relaxed to lack of trust, some people don't speak up. Encourage others to converse by making them feel relaxed, making comments that stimulate conversation or asking open-ended questions such as, "How would you handle this situation?" or "What is your opinion on this project?"

IMAGINE THAT a new staff member appears to be so tense, she practically whispers when she must make a response. You talk to human resources personnel and learn that she was brilliant during her interviews. Since you're an *inner circle* assistant, you invite her to take a walk around the building with you to discuss the training classes she just attended. Once outside, she waxes poetic on what she learned about the new software program. "The pie charts are so easy to do! What we once needed five steps for can now be done in two steps." For the rest of the day, she seems relaxed and doesn't whisper. But this doesn't last. In the first month of her employment, you take her out to lunch, invite her to work out with you in the company gym and take a few more walks around the building. By week five, she's as openly communicative as everyone else. You facilitated this turnaround. Take a bow!

Defining Assertiveness

Many people confuse assertive and aggressive behavior. This is especially true of women, who, until recent years, were often taught to associate passiveness with femininity. As a result, women often are reluctant to take the initiative in the workplace — whether to resolve a conflict, solve a problem or present an idea — for fear of being labeled pushy or obnoxious.

The following activity forces you to take a moment to appreciate the differences. It's not possible to communicate like an *inner circle* assistant if you can't be assertive. And you can't be assertive without a clear understanding of the finer points of the action.

Activity: Use words, phrases or sentences that describe the following. If you can't find the words, check out a thesaurus. The effort should leave you with a complete appreciation of differences.

	What words describe
Passive	
Aggressive	
Assertive	

Tactfully Voicing Opinions

When interviewing a high-level executive for an article on building stellar teams, we discussed the importance of administrative assistants being assertive with their managers. The executive said, "An assistant should be diplomatically assertive with her or his boss. But he or she needs to keep a lid on it and not get out of control!" It's important to voice your opinions. As an *inner circle* assistant, you'll want to really think about how you go about doing that. You must consider everything from the words you use to body language to your tone of voice.

ASSERTION	Confidently expressing what you think, feel and believe. Standing up for your rights while respecting others' rights.
NON-ASSERTION	Inability to express confidently what you think, feel and believe. Allowing others to walk over you.

Benefits of Being Assertive

- *Reduced anxiety*
- *A feeling of control*
- *Increased self-esteem*
- *Confidence*
- *Resolution of the situation*
- *Less stress and wasted time*
- *You choose when to push a situation or not*

Activity: Answer the following questions to determine your level of assertiveness.

1. Think of a recent confrontation at work or a situation in which your needs were not satisfied. How did you behave? What did you say? Were these assertive behaviors and words?

    _____

    _____

    _____

    _____

    _____

2. How could you have expressed yourself or your needs more assertively?

    _____

    _____

    _____

    _____

    _____

You may want to invite a coworker or valued friend to help you evaluate answers. If you go it alone, you may want to make a note of this page and come back to it later, after you've had time to think about it.

Deciding Whether to Assert

Ask Yourself:

- *Will assertiveness improve my relationships and my self-respect?*
- *Will assertiveness prevent or reduce stress?*
- *How important is this situation to me?*
- *How am I likely to feel afterward?*

Levels of Assertion:

Low: Assertion with empathy. You want to show that you recognize the other person's viewpoint or feelings.

Medium: Using "I" messages instead of "you" language will help you retain the goodwill of the person you are standing up to.

High: Sometimes you will have to increase your level of firmness with someone who continues to violate your rights or ignore your stated expectation.

Choosing When to Assert Yourself

Being assertive involves some risk because you aren't guaranteed anything. The outcome is an unknown. You have to be willing to take a chance. However, you have a better chance of having your needs met with assertive action than by being passive or aggressive.

When communicating assertively, it's a good idea to start at the end. State what you want to see happen and then work back from there. Make sure you clearly communicate your needs or desires. When these are communicated in a direct, tactful manner, you most likely will see the result you expected in the beginning.

Start with		Use		Experience
Expected Outcome	⇨	Assertive Communication	⇨	Positive Results

If you are doubtful as to whether to assert yourself in a particular situation, you should weigh the pros and cons.

Think of a situation you are currently experiencing, a person you are in conflict with or feel intimidated by. Decide on specific assertive steps you can take to manage this. What words and behaviors will you use?

Nonverbal Communication When Working Under Pressure

Whether you realize it or not, you are always on stage in the office. People are constantly forming opinions of you. They notice how you dress, sit, stand, talk and even your facial expressions. Because you are so visible to visitors and people in your organization, it is important to reflect a professional image. *Inner circle* performers know how to handle stress and frustration without displaying it on their faces.

How often do you...

	ALWAYS	SOMETIMES	NEVER
Communicate impatience by drumming your fingers or using some other annoying gesture?			
Use a distracting gesture when speaking under pressure?			
Project any of the following without realizing it? Boredom Frustration Fatigue Aggravation			
Sigh when feeling any of the above?			

Be aware of whether or not you embrace the habits just described. If you checked "Sometimes" or "Always," be more conscious of your visual communication.

Communicate Messages Nonverbally

In face-to-face situations, actions speak louder than words. This may or may not be good. It depends on whether your non-verbal message is intentional, to make a certain point, or not intentional. When asserting yourself, you should try to make your body language and facial expression match your verbal communication.

Facial Expression Identities

The following descriptions (e.g., Withholders, Revealers) come from an unknown source. I enhanced them and hope you find them as useful as I do.

WITHHOLDERS (keep feelings from appearing on their faces):
Rather expressionless, Withholders' faces are difficult to read when trying to determine their feelings. To some degree, withholders hinder the flow of communication, because although they may receive nonverbal communication, they seldom send it back in return. (Withholders are probably excellent poker players.)

REVEALERS (the opposite of Withholders):
An administrative assistant said of her boss, "I know the minute she arrives at the office what kind of mood she's in." Another phrased it this way; "She wears her feelings on her face." In each case, the people in the office learned that their boss's face was one of that person's most accurate means of communication.

SUBSTITUTE EXPRESSORS (show different facial expressions from what they are feeling):
Unless you like thinking in reverse, it can be difficult to communicate with such people.

EVER-READY EXPRESSORS (like horses at the starting gate, waiting for the race):
At the slightest reaction to emotion or any other stimulus, these people's faces say it first. Such individuals are often labeled "very expressive."

THREE QUESTIONS: Which one are you? Are you consistent? Is there room for improvement? You may not be the only one who knows the answers. Remember that you're being watched!

Principles of Persuasion

A stellar performance can be sabotaged by power-robbing communication mistakes. The ability to communicate with others, whether it's addressing a group or simply negotiating with a colleague, can be one of your best business assets.

If done correctly, you will get more of what you want, help others see your side and positively motivate others. Here are eight steps to help you get started.

1. To be a good seller, consider the buyer's viewpoint. Help your audience see how he or she will benefit from your idea.
2. Speed up or slow down to match the receiver's speed.
3. Let people know you have their best interests in mind.
4. Things to watch for:
    o Poor body language
    o Bad logic that confuses your audience
    o Stuffy language
5. Do you practice what you preach?
6. Size up the situation before going into a meeting where you plan to persuade.
7. Show an interest in others. When you show an interest in them today, you can persuade them in the future.
8. Offer options.

9. State the benefits of a desired action or direction.

Personal Presentation

Whether you are giving a presentation in front of 500 people or for three people in a meeting, your personal presentation style and speaking abilities will enhance or detract from the point you are trying to make. Presentation skills can also positively or negatively affect how people perceive you.

You present yourself every day, whether you realize it or not. You present yourself on the telephone. You send visual messages to individuals who approach you. Every day you come into contact with many people from all walks of business—coworkers, customers, vendors, suppliers and more. By developing your presentation style and learning tricks of professional speakers, you will:

*   *Become more confident speaking to and in front of others.*
*   *Tactfully handle challenging situations and difficult people.*
*   *Project the image you want to project.*
*   *Generate enthusiasm for your ideas.*
*   *Learn to think on your feet.*
*   *Deliver the message you really want to send.*

The following information is for any individual who wants to make an impact, whether speaking for five minutes or for six hours.

Consider Your Audience

Are you speaking to one manager? A group of managers? Administrative peers? A client? A potential client? Speakers think about their audience as well as the message they want to deliver.

A few questions you can ask yourself are:

1. Who *is* my audience?

2. What is their level of knowledge on the topic I am addressing?

3. What is my purpose in speaking to this person or group? Is it to educate, entertain, motivate, persuade or inform?

4. What is my credibility with this audience?

5. Are there any cultural differences I need to be aware of?

6. Am I presenting this information in an age-appropriate fashion?

7. What is the gender of the person to whom I am speaking or presenting? Based on that, do I need to frame my words differently?

Gather Information

Whether you're presenting on a stage or in your manager's office, you want to make sure you are knowledgeable about the material you present. You may be presenting a new idea to an action team or a group of department heads or giving a major presentation to clients. Whatever your situation, make sure your information is accurate and current. In addition to what you already know about your subject, be sure to do necessary research. You can read books, scan periodicals and magazines, conduct interviews and, of course, use the Internet.

Making Your Thoughts Flow

It's difficult to persuade or convince someone when our thoughts don't flow or connect. Even if you are just delivering an update to someone, you still should take time to make sure your sentences connect and smoothly flow from one thought to the next.

Presenting a Calm Image

Most people are nervous about speaking in front of others. Again, keep in mind that just presenting to a team of administrative peers can be nerve-racking. I remember before I started speaking in front of large groups, I was nervous and had to work at managing my stage jitters. Here are a few sure-fire techniques to help you.

- *Visual yourself delivering your speech with a smile and feeling confident.*
- *Do stress-releasing exercises such as deep breathing.*
- *Think about your topic rather than worry you might forget something.*
- *Think of people without titles or position to help put the audience in perspective.*
- *Practice using any equipment that is a part of your presentation.*
- *Be yourself! Be real.*

You present yourself every day! Studies show that technical competence is not enough to get ahead in the business world. One must reflect powerful self-presentation.

It's worth repeating: Make an impact, whether you are speaking for five minutes or six hours!

You Present Yourself Every Day

Positive self-presentation is the culmination of many things including personal appearance, a sense of humor, making eye contact, attitude, confidence, enthusiasm, stature and good self-image.

Activity: Consider the following, and then think about your own performance.

1. What words come to mind when you think of self-presentation?

_____

_____

_____

2. Think of someone you know who has left a lasting positive impression. What are some of the qualities and traits of this individual?

_____

_____

_____

3. Now think of someone who is lacking in self-presentation skills. What traits about that person turn you off?

_____

_____

_____

4. List daily opportunities or situations in which you can demonstrate professional presentation.

_____

_____

_____

It pays to...

- _Learn to communicate clearly and effectively with all people with whom you come in contact._
- _Remember that self-presentation is just as important outside the office environment._
- _Reflect confidence through your actions and speech._
- _Create and maintain a high profile with those who count._
- _Always put your best foot forward._

- *Avoid personal mannerisms and speech habits that annoy others.*
- *Gain respect by being a star performer.*
- *Accept constructive criticism from your manager(s) with grace and poise.*

Protect Your Company from Security Breaches: Telephone Safety Protocols for the New Century.

Issues of workplace privacy, security and safety take on a new emphasis in today's business world. As our society changes and becomes more global, every employee has a new responsibility to protect both her coworkers and their company. *Being educated on proper telephone protocol is the first line of defense.*

Consider this scenario: You're standing at the reception desk of a major corporation. The receptionist is on the phone with a fellow employee. As you patiently wait for the receptionist to finish the call, you hear her tell her coworker the new security code to get into the building after hours. Not only did you hear this information, but so did the three other people seated in the waiting area. Or let's say a coworker goes on vacation for a week. The assistant proceeds to tell an unfamiliar caller that the employee is away on personal business until the following Tuesday. When your coworker returns home, she finds that her house has been robbed. If you think neither of these scenarios could ever happen in real life, think again. The above two scenarios actually occurred. Did the receptionists of these companies purposely give out private information that could harm the company or its employees? Neither would intentionally breach company confidentiality, but they innocently did so and were not even aware of it. And you may be doing the same thing!

You and others in your company who handle the phone risk jeopardizing the privacy, security, and/or safety of the organization and its employees. The fact is that today, businesses in every sector face new workplace concerns that were nonexistent a mere 10 years ago. While we should not become alarmed about this change of events, we should raise our level of consciousness and become more aware of telephone safety issues.

Training Tips for Telephone Guardians

Excellent telephone skills are vital to business success. And as the business world becomes faster and more uncertain, it is paramount that employees learn to be foolproof guardians of telephone communications. There is a fine line between building rapport with a caller and guarding employee and company information. Use the following suggestions to hone your telephone screening techniques.

1. Elicit information from every caller. Always get the caller's name, organization (or company name) and reason for calling. Other information that may be important is the caller's telephone number, alternate number and mailing address. If the caller says, "He/she has it," don't take the caller's word. Get as much information as possible, accurately document it and then pass it on to the appropriate person. Capturing the necessary information saves those in the company time and ensures accuracy.

2. When relaying messages to their intended recipients, always state your impressions as to the urgency and nature of the call. If the caller says, "I need to speak with Ms. Jones by 3:00 today because I need pertinent information for a report I am writing," then be sure to communicate that to Ms. Jones. Also indicate if you believe the caller was annoyed, frustrated, angry or perplexed. This is important information and helps determine the priority of the return call.

3. Learn to recognize the names and voices of people who call frequently and the nature of their relationship with people you support. Even if a coworker has a close business relationship with a particular caller, don't reveal private information to the caller, such as "She's away for two weeks."

4. Exhibit professionalism and discretion when responding to phone inquiries. Ask key questions that can reveal information regarding the nature of the call. This will contribute to those in your company taking only the calls that are appropriate.

5. Only promise what you can personally deliver. If your manager is away from the office for more than a day, especially if on personal business, never promise the caller that the manager will return a phone call. It may not happen!

A good rule of thumb is to maintain a position of information gatherer rather than information divulger. When in doubt, write all the information you can, including the caller's phone number. Instruct the caller that you will look into the situation and return the call as soon as possible. Anyone phoning with a good and specific purpose in mind will have no problem giving their name and phone number.

NOTE: You may want to obtain my training video *Telephone Protocol: Employee Privacy, Safety and Security*. It reveals vital techniques every telephone guardian should know. For more information, visit our web site at www.officedynamicsltd.com or call 1-800-STAR-139.

Improve Listening Skills

Listening is not only great when confronting problems but extremely useful in many situations throughout the day. It reduces errors and need for rework, and it facilitates understanding of tasks and priorities. Listening opens our minds, increases knowledge and can create opportunities. Here's an exercise you can do alone or with a coworker.

1. Why do you think people don't always listen as well as they should? What kinds of things get in the way internally and externally?

   _____

   _____

   _____

   _____

   _____

2. Do you agree with the following graphic explanation?

   HEARING → PHYSICAL PROCESS → TAKES LITTLE EFFORT

   LISTENING → MENTAL PROCESS →TAKES EFFORT

3. Describe why listening is an important skill to develop.

   _____

   _____

   _____

You Can Develop the Critical Skill of Listening

In this competitive environment, the ability to listen well is a crucial edge. It's one of those *soft skills* that employers look for and clients crave. But it takes consistent practice to achieve the goal of listening (i.e., taking in information). Whether it's in a meeting with clients or with your boss, here's how you can be a better listener:

- *Prepare to listen. It takes a concerted effort to focus on someone else completely. That's why preparation is crucial. Clear your calendar, hold your calls and forget your e-mail.*

- *Write down your goals. What do you want to accomplish by listening? Once you write down your goals and study them, set the list aside physically and mentally. This prevents you from focusing too much on your goals and can help you concentrate on listening.*

- *List your point of view and any prejudices you may have of the person with whom you're meeting. Half the battle of listening is being able to put aside our own points of view enough to really hear another person's point of view. Write your viewpoints and prejudices, and again, put them physically and mentally aside.*

- *Let people know the meeting is important to you. Nod, maintain eye contact and ask short questions to clarify any points. Mind your body language.*

- *Do not interrupt. Interruptions cause individuals to lose their train of thought. The consequences can be misunderstanding and frustration, which are never goals that you're trying to achieve.*

- *After the person is finished speaking, repeat what you think is the essence of her points, using her own words. Then provide an explanation in your own terms. This ensures that you really have understood the other person and allows her to clarify any misunderstanding.*

Communication Tactics: How to Answer Questions

You don't have to be an oracle when it comes to answering questions that come your way on the job. Just give each inquiry —

whether from a boss, coworker or client—your best reply. Follow these tips to giving your best answer each time:

1. **Understand the question.** Miscommunication often occurs when you don't pay close attention to what is being discussed. Make sure you understand what you're being asked, or clarify the question if you're confused.

2. **Don't babble.** If you know the answer to what is being asked, provide it quickly and succinctly rather than spending a lot of time discussing irrelevant information.

3. **Remember that you're the expert.** Don't be intimidated when a manager who has more responsibilities (but less knowledge of the daily working of your position) asks you a question. Back your answer up with facts and details, written and otherwise.

4. **Keep your opinions to yourself.** If you're asked for facts or data, give them. Refrain from adding anecdotal observations to your answer.

5. **Answer the questions.** If you can't immediately answer a question, let the questioner know how soon you can get back to him or her (the sooner the better).

6. **Don't be critical.** Never answer a question with a condescending remark like, "You don't know that?"

7. **Admit when you don't know the answer.** Know when you don't know, but make an extra effort to refer the questioner to sources you know can be of better help.

Course Corrections

When things don't go smoothly, use methods that assist you to get things back on course.

IMAGINE THAT you're working quickly to satisfy a very important customer's wish list. Randall, the warehouse manager, isn't cooperating with you. "We can't put this customer at the head of the line. He'll have to wait!" you're told. You communicate with Randall via e-mail and rarely see him, so you decide to drive to the warehouse and speak with him. When he groans that he's too busy to sit down and talk with you, you realize this isn't such a good idea. "I'll come back later or in the morning, if you prefer," you offer. He agrees to see you early the next morning. You return to your office and prepare e-mail for Randall. "I will be at your office at 7:00 a.m., as requested. You're probably aware that Rex Industries spends over a million dollars annually with our company. You may not know that we disappointed them on a completely unrelated matter last quarter. Our division director has instructed me to make all problems go away. See you in the morning."

Do you recognize the following course corrections? *You hit a roadblock and took an alternate route* by going to the warehouse to confront Randall. *You knew when to walk away or step back*. You demonstrated this by agreeing to come to the warehouse the next morning. *You were persistent and determined and tried again*. You used e-mail to *transmit options and outcomes* (essentially there were none!). The division director outranks Randall, and, in this case, you were the director's emissary.

How to Criticize Effectively

Why not make this one of your goals? We all know that we are more successful when we work well with others and get along with people. There are times that you may find that you need to critique a colleague. No one likes to deliver bad news, especially if it's going to hurt or anger someone. But if you have to criticize a colleague, the following techniques may make your job a little easier.

- *Start off by saying something positive.*
- *Identify the behavior that you want to criticize. Direct your criticism at the action, not the person.*
- *Make criticisms specific. Don't say, "You always miss deadlines." Say, "You missed the project's February 15th deadline."*
- *Don't criticize something that cannot and should not always be changed. For example, foreign accents or physical characteristics remotely related to some business dealings cannot always be changed.*
- *Get right to the point. Don't lecture.*
- *Don't set a tone of anger or sarcasm; both are counterproductive.*
- *Speak in terms of "we" to stress that you want to work out the problem together. Offer to help the person correct the problem.*
- *Show the person you understand his or her feelings. Make sure the other person understands the reason for your criticism.*
- *If you're putting your criticism in writing, write the letter or memo, put it aside, and then look at it a few hours later to make sure you didn't fly off the handle unnecessarily. If you're still satisfied, send the message.*
- *At the end, reaffirm your support for, and confidence in, the person.*

Then & Now — A Looking-Glass View

Then: The support person was inclined to believe, "What I think, I say." He or she couldn't mess up e-mail since it didn't exist. As for telephone techniques, for the most part, the support person acted like a message taker or giver — just following orders. It's fair to conclude that this individual typically served as a conduit, not a player. Of course, some support people have always been mindful of the importance of listening and understanding and adjusting to someone's delivery *style* (e.g., fast, slow, pompous, simple).

Now: The *inner circle* assistant thinks in terms of goal, motive and purpose. *Who is this person? I must be selective about what I divulge.* The *inner circle* professional communicates clearly and concisely, especially when it comes to transmitting e-mail. She's adept with using new technology but doesn't abuse something like voice messaging. She answers the telephone when she's available to do so. (Some support people adapt an "I can't be bothered" approach.) The *inner circle* professional understands that just because machines and modern services are readily available, they should not automatically be used. She knows the power of one-on-one communication techniques, and she uses them to advance her manager's position, her company's position and her own position!

COMPETENCY 6

Office Organization

It starts with you!

Being organized is one of the five skills most requested by managers and employers across the country. (The others are telephone, computer, time management and communication skills.) Today's office environment is busier than ever. Many companies are doing more work with fewer people due to rightsizing, mergers, acquisitions and the flattening of the organizational pyramid. This isn't new but it's ongoing.

Spruce up your filing system.

You can use colorful files to differentiate where information is stored. This increasingly popular method of visual organization enables you to find things quickly.

Examples:

- *If you work for several managers, you might have each manager's files in a different color.*
- *You can also use color to clarify categories of files. For instance, customer files can be blue, complaint files red and you're A-through-Z files green.*

Set up In/Out trays and use them regularly.

Don't let people place things all over your desk or on your chair. Request that they put incoming work and correspondence in your In tray. This way, their things are sure to be seen, and you can then prioritize, delegate and forward items as necessary.

IMAGINE THAT four managers left papers for you in four different places — the top of a file cabinet, on your chair, the corner of your desk and inside your top drawer. Everyone is out to lunch when along come maintenance workers with floor polishers, which are noiseless and do a lovely job on the marble floors in the hallways. But alas, they do create a wind. And for some reason, one of the workers pulls the machine into your carpeted work area, and whoosh, papers take off in many directions. He is alarmed and gathers the papers. He even leaves a note of apology. You spend time sifting through the stack of papers you find when you return. You continue to work, never realizing that the papers left on the file cabinet now rest on the floor behind the cabinet. With only a smidgen of imagination, you can finish this story! The outcome is not good. If *all* the people who leave work for your attention leave it in one secure place, consequences such as this one could be avoided.

Use speed dialing.

If your telephone has speed dialing, add frequently called numbers to its memory. Be sure to do this for your manager, too. Make a list of the names and numbers to keep by your manager's phone for quick reference.

Wherever you go...

Be on the lookout for ways to streamline everything that goes on in your office and at your desk. If purchasing department personnel are unfamiliar with an item you located in a magazine or local office supply store, let them know about availability. Purchase samples of these items if you think that will help to make the point. This is not a one-time activity. Just like perfecting your communication skills, this is an ongoing pursuit.

Organizing your work area. Be careful your workspace does not become storage space.

Make it a place of action. Clear away files and other materials that are only used occasionally. Find another area to store them. If you're at capacity in your file cabinets, go through your cabinets and clean out files. You might be storing things you don't need any more or files that can be sent off to central storage.

Place the items you most frequently use closest to you.

Analyze your activities. Decide which items are used the most and place them in near reach. You might think it only takes 30 seconds to get an item, but add up the number of times you do that in a day and see how much time you can save.

A messy desk signals lack of control and focus.

Appearing busy does not equal appearing productive. Some people assume that if they don't have papers spread all over their desk, others won't think they are busy. It actually sends a message of not being organized or focused; it looks like you don't know what's going on. In some instances, people question whether you are losing things.

Use every inch of space in drawers and cabinets to your advantage.

Here is the order in which to accomplish this:
1. Empty all drawers and storage cabinets.
2. As you empty them, sort items by similar products or categories.
3. Get rid of things you really don't need or want.
4. Before putting items back into the drawers and cabinets, ask yourself:
   - What items do I use most frequently?
   - What items do I rarely use?

- What items do I need nearby that my manager will request?
- What can be stored in file boxes? Visualize and plan where all categories of items will go.
- What should be stored in my manager's office?

Keep similar items together.

For example, cluster different size Post-Its, other types of note pads and message pads and various sizes of paper clips and clamps. By doing this, you save time trying to find the items you need. If you keep your supplies orderly, you will know when you are getting low on a particular supply and can order it.

Then & Now — A Looking-Glass View

Then: Organization was important, but it was more leisurely. Typically, a support person came to work and his or her desk, files, supplies and office furniture were *just there*. The philosophy was more of an "Ours is not to reason why" philosophy.

Now: Office organization is critical because of the faster pace in the workplace. Technology and people's expectations contribute to the speed. Moreover, you may be supporting multiple managers — something that has come about in response to running leaner and meaner organizations. Without careful organization, you'd be sunk. The *inner circle* professional finds sources, supplies and files at a speed that could match Superman's prowess. And she plays a key role in perfecting office organization. She frequently has the power of the purse — access to company budgets — something that was unheard of *then*. Since the *inner circle* professional is both smart and creative, she or he elevates the importance of office organization to anything but a leisurely pursuit.

COMPETENCY 7

Problem Solving

Employees no longer have the luxury of just turning over problems to managers or business owners. Long gone are the days when you could see or hear a problem, tell your manager, go back to your little corner and wait for the solution. You are faced with challenging situations requiring you to think creatively and make decisions nearly every day.

The tips, techniques and methods you discover in this chapter will not be used for every problem you encounter. However, they are often useful for solving major problems, when working in teams or when supervising other employees.

Think of problem solving as a process having three stages. If any one of these stages is skipped, the outcome may not be as effective or as long-lasting as it could be.

Stage I: Recognition	1. Clearly state the problem. 2. List negative effects. 3. Assemble relevant information. 4. Write five to 10 possible solutions.
Stage II: Decision Making	1. List the positive or negative outcomes of each solution. 2. Select the best one.
Stage III: Implementation	1. Consider how you will present this information to those involved: communication styles; format (verbal, written, timing).

Become a Self-motivated Employee

In today's lean workplace, every employee must take initiative in his or her job. That means employees should know how to work independently, without constant supervision. Here are some suggestions on how to become a self-motivated employee.

1. **If you've got a complaint, think of a solution.** Don't just go to a supervisor with a complaint. Go to the supervisor, outline a problem and then offer solutions.
2. **Communicate clearly.** The chances of miscommunications are great. Even if you're careful, your audience may not necessarily hear or read what you intended to say. Encourage questions to ensure that you are clearly understood.

3. **Take on the characteristics of a model company.** Ideal companies provide stability, consistency and flexibility. In turn, they also have model employees who set the standards. Reflect those values in your work.

4. **Brainstorm by fax.** If you need other people's opinions on a project, but they're in different locations, try using the fax machine. E-mail subject headings are quickly scanned and sometimes the eye overlooks an important message. Try faxing your questions, especially when they're timely. Your audience will have a physical reminder to get back to you.

The Absence of Good Judgment

Good judgment is an important skill to develop, if that is even possible to do. Throughout the day, you make decisions. You determine the manner in which you want to handle a project, the way you want to respond to a coworker, the order in which you will do your work and even whether you should present a new idea to colleagues or withhold your idea. If you were to look up the word "judgment" in a thesaurus, you would find some of the following words:

analysis	logic
conclusion	assessment
decision	mind
conviction	attitude
taste	estimate
belief	wisdom

Interestingly, at the time a person makes a decision, she or he feels it's the right one. Reflect on an incident where you felt you made the right decision. At the time you made it, you probably felt it was a good one. However, a day or week or month later, you may have thought about how you could have handled it better or come up with a different decision.

Ask Yourself...

1. What determines or truly constitutes good judgment?

    Try to add to this list: Experience, maturity, morals and values, asking "What's best for the company?" (Time and outcome will tell whether you made the right decision.)

    _____

    _____

    _____

    _____

2. Who determines whether a decision was good or not?

    Try to add to this list: We, the receivers of the information, the ones affected by the decision and the customer. (A happy boss or a satisfied customer confirms positive results.)

    _____

    _____

    _____

    _____

Tapping into Your Creative Energy

Dr. Edward de Bono, creativity educator, says that a company will no longer survive by staying in its present state. "As competition intensifies, so does the need for creative thinking. It is no longer enough to do the same thing better. It is no longer enough to be efficient and solve problems. Far more is needed. Business needs creativity both on the strategic level and on the front line to make the shift that competitive business demands—from administration to true entrepreneurship."

That's where you come in. You are on the front line. And that is a great place to be. You see a lot of activity not only within your area but throughout the organization. People who work on the front lines tend to have a very good perspective of what really is going on, how coworkers feel, and have a pulse on internal activities. This gives you a wonderful opportunity to use your creative talents to help your organization become more competitive, be proactive in problem solving and possibly prevent costly customer service faux pas.

Elaine Biech, author of *Creativity & Innovation*, states: "Most companies are going through many changes. Many have recently invested in state-of-the-art technology. Many have plans to broaden their customer base. Some have redesigned the business processes by which they operate. Companies have flattened, de-layered, teamed, reengineered, process improved and reorganized. These changes require a new way of thinking: creativity to spawn the idea and risk taking to push the idea to obtain innovative results."

Don't think the above comments are for your company's management team only! They apply to you and everyone else in your organization, whether they work in the mailroom or in the boardroom. The employees are the ones who are affected positively or negatively by flattening, delayering or reorganizing. But these can also be seen as wonderful opportunities for growth and challenge. These are the kinds of work situations that sort out the tough-minded from the soft-minded employees.

As Elaine said, "It takes creativity to give birth to an idea and then risk taking to push the idea through." When was the last time you truly used your creativity? Interestingly, scientists believe that we use only two to three percent of our brains. The creative thought process is based upon the idea that your brain has the ability to create an infinite number of ideas, combinations and relationships.

Team: Making Problems Transparent to Management

The old paradigms are quickly going out the window. Organizations today expect their employees to be responsible and accountable for their own actions and even their department's or team's actions. All employees must help their organizations streamline, cut costs, gain new customers and maintain a competitive edge. Employees are being challenged to develop new ideas and be catalysts for change. As upper management shifts their ways of interacting with employees, employees must learn to handle problems and even bring answers and new ideas to the table.

Old work paradigms said:

- *"Management is responsible for solving problems."*
- *"Managers are the only ones who should make decisions."*
- *"If you are an employee, bring your problem to your manager and let him or her solve it."*
- *"If there were a customer service issue, it's the company's problem, not mine."*
- *"I can't save the company money. I only spend it."*
- *"It's not my problem we don't have more business."*

(NOTE: Read the Then and Now sidebar at the end of this chapter, too.)

Here, again, you can use your creativity. Every day you have the chance to solve problems, create change and make things better. As important as that is, so is building a strong relationship with the people you support. You will become a more valuable asset when you use your creativity to resolve conflicts and tactfully handle problems instead of turning them over to your manager. We have noticed in our office, though, something very interesting: We all work independently as far as handling our own work loads, and we all have our own areas of responsibilities. However, we work like a finely-tuned car together. For example, when we're looking for ways to host a successful conference, we bring all our talents to the table. The results are outstanding!

Strategy

Although creativity is usually considered spontaneous and intuitive, you can still have a little strategy behind it. The reason is that we have several blocks that get in the way of our creativity.

You can have a strategy as to how you will get around these blocks if you experience them today or in the future. As you look at this list, ask yourself these questions:

- *Is this me?*
- *Do I experience this creativity block?*
- *How often do I experience this block?*
- *How has this block hindered my being more successful in the workplace?*
- *What will I do to overcome this block?*

Common Creativity Blocks

- *Fear of making a mistake, failing or taking a risk.*
- *Inability to tolerate ambiguity; overriding desires for security, order.*
- *Preference for judging ideas rather than generating them.*
- *Inability to relax, incubate and sleep on it.*
- *Lack of challenge; problem fails to engage interest.*
- *Excessive zeal; overmotivation to succeed quickly.*
- *Lack of access to areas of imagination.*
- *Lack of imaginative control.*
- *Pessimism.*

Then & Now — A Looking-Glass View

Then: The support person saw the problem, brought it to the boss and that was about it. He or she was told what to do. Essentially, it was a process of reacting. This individual didn't perceive *running the business.*

Now: The *inner circle* professional *looks for problems*! He or she comes up with solutions. The *inner circle* professional takes time to consider options, gathers information and presents the problem to the boss. If the boss doesn't have a solution to the challenge, the *inner circle* professional stands ready to offer one. This individual goes one step further; he or she anticipates. This dynamite support person is future-focused. That involves thinking about impact down the road. What will this mean in three, four or five weeks? The *inner circle* professional is definitely engaging his or her brain since the focus in on running the business.

COMPETENCY 8

Professional Behavior & Image

According to a Chinese proverb, "The best strategy in life is diligence." These simple words deliver a powerful truth. They also help to explain why this chapter is the largest chapter in the book!

You develop and hone countless skills to gain entrance to the *inner circle* of your profession, but none is more vital than your *continued effort to perfect yourself*. Be diligent, conscientious, attentive, painstaking, hard-working and meticulous. Apply this rule to all that you master. It's the underlying theme to your success. It deserves a *big* place in your life and therefore gets a *big* chapter.

Outstanding office professionals not only have excellent business skills but excellent interpersonal skills. They realize these are as important to their business success as any of their basic work duties. While many office professionals have become technically proficient, they have not focused on their people skills.

What do you do all day in some way, shape or form?
You interact with people!

Even if you're sending an e-mail message, that message is going to be read and judged by a person. When you leave a voice message, a person is going to listen to it.

I have repeatedly seen people overlooked for promotions or kept away from top positions because of poor interpersonal skills. If you think they don't matter, you had better think again. You are exposed to a multitude of people inside and outside the organization. Your business and personal success will depend on your ability to handle situations and people with tact, poise and discretion.

Start the New Year with an Open Mind

Three years ago, I wrote an article about keeping an open mind for our New Year issue of *StarQuest* and later reproduced it in an issue of *Office Life* (both were publications of Office Dynamics, Ltd.). The message appears to be timeless and worthwhile for anyone hoping to reach the top of that ladder of success. Accordingly, I'm sharing it with you now:

As a new year begins, our enthusiasm and energy usually grow. We most often look forward to a new year and think about how we can make it better than the previous year. Setting goals, breaking old habits and developing new habits (like getting on an exercise program) are common.

The one habit I've been working at for several years is keeping an open mind. It's easy to say, "I'm open-minded" or to tell others, "You need to have an open mind." It's hard, though, to keep an open mind when ideas, systems and others' beliefs aren't in line with yours. Embracing a desire for open-mindedness is essential for personal and professional growth. When a colleague or manager presents an idea foreign to your own thinking, instead of passing judgment immediately, listen and at least take some time to consider the idea. Say to yourself, "I will give this idea a try."

Every day, you have the opportunity to learn from others, whether a coworker, vendor, client or just someone you casually meet. Without an open mind, you will miss many opportunities to grow and become even better.

What does it mean to have an open mind?

- *Being ready for anything.*
- *Not limiting yourself to your views.*

- *Understanding what change might bring about.*
- *Listening without judgment.*
- *Being tolerant.*

How can you keep an open mind?

- *Be receptive.*
- *Put yourself in the other person's shoes.*
- *Don't be afraid to try something new.*
- *Realize that it is okay to be different.*
- *See opportunity and challenge yourself.*

Change is essential for growth. We can't always think of everything ourselves. Experiences, backgrounds, geographic locations, upbringing, careers and friends limit us. Although we grow from these, we need more than that to expand our horizons for a brighter future.

The Challenge of Change

A natural reaction to change is fear of the unknown. People would much rather stay in their comfort zones, where they feel safe and secure. Change that you initiate, however, can be challenging and rewarding. No mere accident of fate determines who thrives on change; it is a process totally within your control.

There are two kinds of change—welcome/wanted and unwelcome/unwanted. Changes that you initiate are much easier to deal with than changes that are forced upon you, but either way, change can be scary.

Change comes in different sizes. There are little changes, like a new neighbor or a detour on the way to work or your favorite barber moving away. Then there are major changes, like divorce, death or moving out of state. And some fall in between.

Activity: List what you consider to be:

Minor Changes	Major Changes

These lists are subjective. What you consider major changes may be minor to another person and vice versa. For example, I have moved out of state more times than I care to admit. Years ago, my older sister moved from a home she had lived in for many years. Although she only moved to a nearby suburb, this experience was traumatic for her. To me, it was not a major event, because I had made so many major moves.

Take the Stress Out of Change

The world of work changes rapidly, and it's up to you to adjust. Of course, change is stressful, but it needn't get the best of you. Try these strategies to help you cope with a changing work environment and beat back the stress.

Write down the pros and cons of an impending change. Much of what gets us worrying about change is not knowing what the change will mean. For example, guess at the potential ramifications of a company merger insofar as your job is concerned and you'll be able to minimize your fears. List the downsides to the changes, and list the potential upsides. Don't just assume the worst without looking at the positives the change has to offer.

- *Do your homework. If your company is merging, it would behoove you to do a little research on the culture of the other company. Find out who's who in the power structure. Arm yourself with information about the people you'll be working with.*
- *Network, network, network. When you find that your team is being restructured, don't wait for others to invite you to introduce*

yourself. Be proactive and get to know as many of the new workers as you can. As you talk to new coworkers, you may get a better understanding of new opportunities or expectations. And taking the initiative lets others know you're willing to adjust to changes.

- **Contribute right away.** *The best way to show that you're capable and flexible is to get started on projects on which you can work. Keep managers up to date on your involvement in plans or projects.*

Winning People Over to Change

You've got a great opportunity to make the way some things are done at work more efficient and effective. But it's going to be hard to get your coworkers' support. So how do you prepare to pitch your ideas and diminish confrontation? Here are a few rules that'll smooth the way:

- **Know the sensitive issues.** *Never walk into a presentation without considering which issues will come up. Try to anticipate others' concerns and reactions, and draw up a game plan to handle them.*
- **Focus on the issues.** *Don't take objections personally. Focus on the issues and your goals, not the person who is disagreeing with you.*
- **Gain understanding.** *Listen carefully to get to the bottom of objections and differences of opinion so you can move toward resolving the issue.*
- **Ask for help.** *Seek the advice of mentors and people you respect. You'll need the backup when you face resistance from colleagues.*
- **Choose your battles.** *Remember that not all issues carry the same weight or importance. Choose your battles, and keep your focus on winning people over to change.*

How to Succeed in the Workplace

Your future at work depends on one thing: taking charge of your own career. As we move into the future, jobs as we once knew them have been transformed. In some companies, there are no titles, no corner offices and no clear hierarchy. You are required to be not only an individual contributor but also a team member and innovator. Here are some tips to help you become truly indispensable.

- ***Think like an entrepreneur.*** *See yourself as the president of You, Inc. Don't just think of yourself as working for someone else. Learn to take responsibility and be accountable for your actions and decisions. Be a creator of your work environment. Quit waiting for management to create the culture. Be a catalyst in making good things happen where you work.*

- ***Think "teams."*** *See beyond you and your manager as a team. Think of your department colleagues as your teammates. See people in other departments as part of the bigger team. A company should be a constellation of talent. As each person becomes better at what he or she does and shares their successes with each other, each department becomes stronger. As each department becomes more effective, the entire organization excels.*

- ***Be a problem solver.*** *Long gone are the days of running to management with problems and letting them solve them. In the new work environment, you will have to tackle problems inside and outside your immediate area. When you see a problem, take ownership. Think of several solutions, evaluate possible outcomes, select one and move forward.*

- ***Take risks.*** *Taking risks can be scary. When you take a risk, you usually are not guaranteed of the outcome. But if you never take a risk – push your limits – you will never know your true potential.*

- **Seek feedback.** *All of us have blind spots. While we may think we know all our strengths and weaknesses, others see us in a different light. Encourage feedback from your manager, colleagues, customers and others who interact with you regularly. Once you receive their feedback, work on a plan for improvement.*

Attitude -- Keep Your Positive Focus

Remember: The most important attribute of a successful person is attitude with a positive slant. Here is a list of ways to keep your mind focused on the positive side of every event. Post this list next to your desk, in your car, at home by the mirror and, if necessary, inside your laptop case.

- *Keep your mind fixed on your goals.*
- *Laugh in the face of adversity.*
- *Get excited by every achievement, no matter how small.*
- *Never dwell on misfortunes; they are mental depressants.*
- *Associate with people who have a positive outlook.*
- *Treat each experience as another step toward your dreams.*
- *Commitment action and self-esteem determine your outcomes.*
- *Consistency is not a luxury; it's a necessity!*

Voice Mail Skill

Let's freshen up voice mail skills! The telephone is the most critical business tool. It seems to be the one skill people feel they don't have to nurture. I polled 75 workshop participants on their likes and dislikes of voice mail. Here was the general consensus:

LIKES	DISLIKES
Flexibility to leave desk	Incomplete messages
Accessible from other phones	Unable to communicate urgency
Receiver can get messages anytime	Long messages
Allows receiver time to get answers before returning phone call	Not having calls returned
Can leave messages not needing a response	Talking to a machine
	Messages not updates

Voice mail in a business is different from an at-home answering machine and gives you an opportunity to show your professionalism. Refer to the guidelines outlined in Office Communications.

Do You Implode or Explode?

Our minister is a pretty smart person as well as a good speaker. In a recent sermon, he talked about conflict, attitudes and how some people hold everything in while others let their anger out.

As you think about renewing everything from your skills to your health, consider the importance of replenishing your attitude. Conflict affects our attitude, which impacts our ability to be productive. Conflict is destructive if not positively handled. It damages peace and orderliness within us as relationships are broken. Our ability to trust people is hindered, and we pull away rather than build relationships.

C = closed-minded
O = opinionated
N = negative attitude
F = frequent frustrations
L = low self-esteem
I = ignorance
C = creates hostile environment
T = temperamental

Now is the time to resolve conflicts or any long-time resentment. Conflict actually can be good if we use positive energy and strategies to deal with it. Here are a few quick ideas:

1. Listen carefully in order to understand the other person's point of view.
2. Solicit ideas from the other person. Ask, "How do you see us working better together?"
3. Be clear on the real issue of conflict. Make sure it just isn't your perception.
4. Stick to the facts when confronting someone.
5. Acknowledge the other person's good points.
6. Maintain the other person's self-esteem.
7. Make every effort to approach the other person directly.
8. Be open and honest; don't hint.

To learn more, I highly recommend the book *Everyday Business Etiquette* by Marilyn Pincus. The book is available from Office Dynamics, Ltd. by calling 1-800-STAR-139.

Introductions	Phone	Email	Choice of words
Don't leave anyone out. If you don't know a person's name, ask for it.	Respect privacy. Be cautious about giving information to someone you don't know.	Originate e-mail only when necessary. Resist using it simply because it's available.	Simple words such as "hello" and "goodbye" help to demonstrate civility.
Take the initiative if no one else does. Introduce yourself.	Assist a caller to get to the point by asking questions. "How can I help?"	A subject line is like a headline. Let readers know what to expect.	Use "please" and "thank-you" when you write or speak.
Ask for clarification, if necessary, so that you pronounce names correctly.	Keep conversations brief.	Confidential information or proprietary information should not be sent via e-mail.	If you must interrupt a conversation, wait for a pause. Say, "Excuse me" and then wait.
Smile! Speak clearly.	Keep promises or don't make them.	Use the company system for business.	Use words people can understand.
Offer information that helps conversation to proceed. "Sam Jones is a jet pilot."	Repeat numbers and offer to spell unfamiliar words.	Be positive and polite.	People do business with people they like. Avoid words that agitate.

Your Attitude Controls Your Altitude

It's true. Our attitude will move us forward, keep us stagnant or move us backward. Attitude can...

- *Create or hinder success.*
- *Make or break relationships.*
- *Help us be more efficient or slow us down.*
- *Increase or decrease our effectiveness with others.*
- *Reflect a positive or negative tone on the telephone.*

Our attitude is one of our most precious possessions. While we think others or situations control our attitudes, they don't. It's nice to be able to blame a bad attitude on what someone said to us. Or it's easy to say we have a bad attitude because of a situation at work.

The truth is that *life happens and people are just people*! We choose the attitude we want to take. And that is the good news! No matter what happens, no matter what someone says to you or how that boss criticized your work, you get to choose how you want to respond. Just remember that if you choose to respond negatively, then you will have a negative domino effect on the next thing or person. And possibly even the next.

Self-Management as an Attitude

Attitudes are as important to your professional success as the skills you bring to your job. Your attitude can dramatically affect your productivity, interactions with others and reactions to situations. Your attitude frames the picture you have of the world and of other people. Rather than allowing people or events to shape your attitude, you have the power within you to determine the attitude you want to embrace. That is called having a self-managing attitude.

The first goal is for you to gain an overview of the self-management philosophy and what it encompasses. From that point, we'll look at self-management as an attitude that all star achievers should want to embrace.

The concepts I'm about to share are simple but profound. As you begin this journey of new awareness, give yourself time — to understand, to process, to incorporate, to make it a part of your life.

Nationwide, people who have grasped self-management and have made it a part of their life have:

- *Learned to enjoy each moment of their life.*
- *Realized that they didn't have to make any major changes.*
- *Become more productive.*
- *Had free-flowing thought processes.*
- *Been more creative.*
- *Found that other people's negative attitudes and behaviors don't have to affect them.*
- *Maintained a calm mindset, even when it's storming.*
- *Discovered that even the most serious circumstances can be serenely handled.*
- *Found joy in their work.*

Characteristics of Successful Self-Managers

There truly are individuals who are successful self-managers. That means being able to manage one's attitudes about situations, events and people. It is being conscious of one's thinking when it is becoming harmful. Self-managing is sometimes a concentrated effort, and other times it just flows.

Quality of life is important to successful self-managers. They realize that the quality of their lives will be in direct proportion to the quality of their thinking. We can take this one step further and say that the quality of the products or services these people deliver as employees is in direct proportion to the quality of their thinking while providing those services or working on those products.

Example: Bill is working on a 20-page report that is due in one week. Because Bill handles challenges positively, he gets his report done on time with no errors in a professional format.

Having the awareness that attitude affects well-being, judgment and creativity is important to successful self-managers. Negative attitudes can be tremendously damaging. Positive attitudes contribute to our success in our day-to-day work.

Example: Mary is on the telephone with a client who is not totallysatisfied with the service her company provided. Mary listens to understand the client's perspective, keeps a positive attitude, does not become defensive and uses her creativity to come to a win-win conclusion.

Uncomfortable feelings alert self-managers. Instead of avoiding or putting off feelings of frustration due to unmet expectations or poor communication, self-managers deal with the situation. They approach the individual with whom they are in conflict or disagreement in a thoughtful, caring way.

Example: Penny Pendleton, vice president of corporate strategy, was disappointed in the project her assistant worked on for her. Penny thought she was clear in her expectations for the project. Rather than hold her feelings of disappointment in, she approached her assistant in an understanding and caring way to find out what went wrong.

Putting problems on the back burner is a good idea when self-managers, for some reason, can't come up with the answer.

Example: Jim has been tasked with cutting office supply expenses by 15 percent and presenting his solution in two weeks at the department staff meeting. Five business days have passed and Jim seems to hit a brick wall whenever he sits down to work on it. He finally decides to just step away from the task for a few days. While getting ready for work one morning, suddenly an idea comes to mind on how to cut expenses.

Listening to understand is one of the greatest strengths of self-managers. They not only listen to a person's ideas and facts, they listen for the speaker's feeling and emotions.

Example: Rebecca, an administrative assistant, participates on an action team in her area. The team is working on redefining the administrative and secretarial positions in the company. From time to time, Rebecca disagrees with some of the other team members. However, she doesn't express her opinion until she has fully listened to the speaker's ideas and understands their feelings behind them.

Getting Emotions Under Control

At work, we are under pressure like never before, and sometimes, our anger and frustration get the best of us.

Quick Facts:

- *Business has changed tremendously over the past decade.*
- *Downsizing, technology and increased competition have a tremendous effect on employees.*
- *All office workers are trying to cope with the crises that arise in their personal and professional lives.*
- *Every business and organization is comprised of individuals with unique personalities and backgrounds.*
- *Every organization has its own distinctive culture.*
- *"Being smart at office politics is an important part of being able to survive and reduce your stress levels." (Christine A. Leatz, M.S.W.)*
- *The sea of information is causing information overload.*

Self-Managing Attitudes

- *Focus on today and do the best you can in each moment.*
- *Each day, focus on the good things in your life.*
- *If you volunteer for a project, be 100-percent committed to giving your best.*
- *Use self-management to cope with crises.*
- *Add "putting things on the back burner" as a problem-solving method.*
- *Put things in proper perspective.*
- *Handle challenges positively.*
- *Acknowledge uncomfortable feelings.*

Weapons to Win

There is one tactic that will truly slay Dragons. Face them! Dragons won't go away unless you learn to face them in a positive fashion. Here are suggestions on how to face Dragons head on. Remember, this also applies to those times when you are your own Dragon.

Act—Don't React!

Reaction cycles never end. Only when you decide to think and act independently will you progress toward your goal. Reacting is responding to your immediate feeling. It puts you at the mercy of the Dragon.

Acting is proactive. It's thinking through what is happening and taking positive steps. It puts you in control. This makes you feel good about what could be a negative situation. You probably will respond differently to a situation if you act rather than react to it.

Educate the Dragon

Some Dragons don't even know they are Dragons. Think about how, when and where you can approach the Dragon to talk about his or her behaviors. Try to help the Dragon see the negative impact of these behaviors, and provide positive techniques the Dragon can use to combat them.

Confront the Dragon

There are certain Dragon species you have to confront head on. You have to be careful how and when you confront them and what words you use. You want the Dragon to know that you are serious and want the Dragon-like behavior to stop. Keep in mind the following:

1. Make sure you have all the facts about the situation.
2. Have a plan before confronting the Dragon face to face. Decide when and where you will talk to the Dragon, how you will do it and what you will say.
3. Use non-threatening language. You don't want to lower your standards and be like the Dragon. You can make your point by selecting appropriate words and being firm.
4. Let the Dragon know by your speech, body language and facial expression that you mean business.
5. Make eye contact with the Dragon.
6. Let the Dragon know that his/her current behavior is unacceptable.
7. State your expectations for future behavior.
8. If it happens again, confront the Dragon again.

Focus on Changing Yourself Instead of Others

A good first step is communicating with the Dragon. Informing someone and offering suggestions is sometimes helpful, because people don't always see their negative attitude or behavior. In the final analysis, however, every adult does as he or she chooses. When you can't change a situation or a person's behavior, look at changing yourself. You can still control your attitude.

Take Independent Steps Toward Your Goals

Determine what your goals are and write them down. List the one thing you can do toward achieving those goals each day. Doing this combines the winning strategies of independent action, self-change, positive control and accomplishment.

Setting and achieving goals give you a sense of accomplishment. This is a positive feeling. When you feel good about who you are and what you do, it naturally flows over to others.

Enjoy What You Are Doing

If you feel bored, stagnant or overwhelmed, maybe you are not putting enough positive energy into your work. Decide to look for the good in your job and how to make it more fun. Be creative and you will have more energy. Find challenge and enjoyment in your work by doing it differently, finding a better or easier way and doing it to the best of your ability and with pride. If you've been in your position for a long time, you might be feeling unchallenged. You can change that in a moment.

Take Control

Maybe you cannot control how much work or what kind of work is given to you, but you can control the order in which you do it, the manner or format and how you organize it. You can control how you accept responsibility. Can you rise to the challenge when given certain tasks, or do you complain?

Being organized, knowledgeable and positive about work and people gives you a sense of control.

Are You a Dragon?

You don't enjoy working with a Dragon, right? It's just as important to make sure you aren't a Dragon to your coworkers.

Activity: Rate yourself on the qualities below by placing an X on the scale. Do you always do these things? Could you be a Dragon without realizing it?

Rarely	Frequently	
☐	☐	Focus on my job; avoid distractions
☐	☐	Cooperate as a team player
☐	☐	Avoid complaining
☐	☐	Show motivation for my job
☐	☐	Keep confidential information to myself
☐	☐	Show respect for coworkers
☐	☐	Avoid gossiping about others
☐	☐	Produce high-quality work
☐	☐	Help coworkers when they need it
☐	☐	Do what I say I will do
☐	☐	Share necessary information

You can be a Dragon to yourself when you:
- *Don't focus on the job.*
- *Let others damage your attitude.*
- *Lack assertiveness.*
- *Don't see your own potential.*
- *Try to please everyone.*
- *Fall into Dragon-like habits.*

- *Lack confidence.*
- *Take criticism personally.*

You can do more harm to yourself with negative thinking than any outside Dragon. It is your thought process and attitude that control your internal Dragon. You have the power at any time to tame your Dragon and put out the fire of any Dragon-like qualities.

Don't Blow It — Deal With It

Remember that you can easily blow your career by losing your cool at work. So know ahead of time what might cause such incidents, and think about ways to deal with them civilly and compassionately:

1. You feel left out. Lack of acceptance among peers provokes anger and hurt feelings, potentially limiting your effectiveness on the job. What can you do to feel more a part of a team effort?

2. Your boss nitpicks. A critical boss is one of the key frustrations for employees, who often adopt a do-no-more-than-necessary attitude. But this can lead to more criticism and start a vicious cycle. Can you find ways to calmly deal with criticism?

3. You don't get the recognition you deserve. While management guide after management guide touts the necessity of showing appreciation to employees, employees often don't get credit for the hard work and extra hours they put into their jobs. How can you help your manager take notice of your efforts?

4. You're the subject of a vicious rumor. False rumors are hurtful, and employees fear they will cause irreparable damage to their reputations or careers. Do you know who you should talk with to combat a hurtful or harmful rumor?

5. You have an incompetent boss. Most of us want to admire and respect the people we work for, but when that person is inept, we risk losing our enthusiasm for our jobs and respect for the company. Can you find a mentor or build a support system of your own at work?

Think Before You Retaliate

It's almost instinctive to yell back or to be offended at someone who is yelling at us, be it a coworker or a boss, but yelling back or arguing accomplishes little. It can destroy a business relationship and certainly dims your professional image. So before you respond to a verbal attack, keep these things in mind:

- *Figure out what's really going on. In each of the following cases, compassion – not retaliation – is in order.*
- *Everyone is liable to blow up during a rough day at work. If the person yelling at you isn't known as a chronic jerk, then consider that the source of the blowup is due to other reasons and not personal.*
- *Consider that some people are just socially inept and know no other way to communicate than to yell.*
- *Then there are some people who crave the attention and know that yelling is one way to get it.*
- *Listen before you leap to conclusions. Assume first that what a person is saying is true. More often than not, we tend to start making a list of what's wrong with a person and miss the opportunity to really find out what's at issue. At that point, no one is listening to what the other is saying.*

- *Stay neutral. Instead of adding fuel to the argument by yelling back, deflect the hostilities. Don't walk away; instead, demonstrate a neutral position. Answer in a calm, steady voice or give an inane answer. It usually stops an argument cold.*

Develop Strong People Skills

Think people skills—think strategy:

- *You should have a strategy for determining which people skills you need to develop.*
- *All inner circle professionals have a strategy for when and how to use their people skills.*
- *Star achievers know that people skills give them the edge, which is part of their career strategy.*

Problem Solving:

Being good at solving problems is often just a matter of looking at things from several different angles. Instead of concentrating solely on your immediate duties, practice identifying some of the roadblocks that impede the work flow in your department. Even if it's a small problem, try to come up with an innovative solution. Strong organizing skills can enhance your problem-solving abilities.

Ethics:

Some skills and qualities just can't be taught. They're best absorbed by observation over time. Take note of the way people you admire use their expertise in diplomacy, courtesy and honesty in various situations.

Open-mindedness:

The office of the future requires innovation and flexibility. That can take practice. As you go about your daily routine, try being as open as possible to other approaches, even when you believe your way is best.

Persuasiveness:

Consider taking courses in communication and negotiation at your local college, and read, read, read. Review the styles of writers in top national publications for insight into how to communicate clearly and concisely. Effective communication is a two-way street; it's important to practice being a good listener.

Leadership:

Sometimes, learning by doing is the best approach. To build leadership abilities, volunteer to head a committee with a local nonprofit, civic or professional organization. Such experiences outside of the workplace can be an effective way to learn more about accountability as well as how to manage and motivate people.

Educational Interests:

Your education is never complete. Embrace the concept of lifelong learning by keeping pace with new trends in your field and in technology.

Interacting With Coworkers

Your team can overcome personality conflicts — and boost productivity — by keeping the following points in mind:

1. You don't have to be best buddies to work together. Even if you don't socialize after work, you can still have perfectly productive working relationships with team members.

2. No one's perfect. Sure, some of your teammates will get on your nerves, but you, too, may rub people the wrong way. Remind everyone that all members deserve to be treated with courtesy and respect, despite any personality differences.

3. You may have more in common than you think. Even with your differences, you share something significant with coworkers — a stake in the success of your team

and company. View colleagues as allies in your quest to achieve goals.

4. Accept, even encourage, differing opinions. The results can generate fresh thinking and give you a new perspective on your job.

5. Effective teamwork takes planning. Don't let teammates go with the flow and hope for the best. Work with members to set clear-cut goals. Discuss them together, write them down and distribute copies to the group.

6. Measure progress. Being aware of the team's accomplishments will inspire everyone to continue working together.

Source: *Leadership from the Front Lines* (Bureau of Business Practice)

Dealing with Difficult People

- *Expect the unexpected.*
- *Take a short break before confronting the individual.*
- *Don't act like a victim.*
- *Remind yourself that this person may just be having a bad day.*
- *Ask questions to clarify the problem.*
- *Listen.*
- *Use humor.*

Control your attitude.

When dealing with difficult people, the most important thing to remember is that you have ultimate control of your attitude. You always have a choice as to how to respond to a given individual. You can get upset and frustrated, or you can remain calm and handle that person with tact.

Stay calm, cool and collected.

Try counting to 10, taking a break, walking away from the situation or even putting the person on the phone on hold for a short time. These techniques work, because they break you away from the situation, giving you time to think what to do.

Use your brain and not your heart; but have heart.

In other words, do not use emotions to handle a difficult person. When you use emotion, you are just reacting. Instead, use your mind to deal with the negative person or situation. When you do this, you are in control.

Attack the problem and not the person.

It never does any good to attack people. Obviously, something happened that caused the conflict. Get to the issue and focus on it rather than on the person.

Strategies for Cooperative Conflict

Weigh the situation and consequences.

Evaluate the situation and think about the consequences of your actions. See beyond the immediate. Anticipate what could happen and whether you can live with that. Then act in a positive, confident manner.

Listen.

Listen carefully in order to understand the other person's point of view. Block out your own thoughts, judgments and priorities, and listen to the other person's concerns and feelings.

Solicit ideas from each other.

Ask the other person questions like, "What do you think the problem is?" "How do you see us working better together?" or "How can I help you accomplish your goals?"

Define the problem.

Are you clear on the real issue of conflict, or is it just your perception? Ongoing communication helps clarify each person's perception of the situation, ensuring that the problem is clearly defined.

Use facts only.

Stick to the facts when confronting someone. You will get more positive results when you deal with the facts than with the emotions around them.

Acknowledge the other person's strengths.

Objectively look at the situation and acknowledge the other person's good points. Keep them in mind while dealing with the issue.

Maintain each other's self-esteem.

It's harmful to belittle others; it diminishes your professional image. When confronting colleagues, make sure you communicate in a way that allows them to save face.

Talk to each other, not about each other.

Make every effort to approach the other person directly. Don't talk behind someone's back. Have the courage to talk to her. This gives you an opportunity to work on solutions.

Listen for underlying issues.

Sometimes, what we think is the problem really isn't. When the other person is speaking, listen for any hidden issues. Try to get to the heart of the conflict so you can deal with it.

Be open and honest; don't hint.

- Use assertive communication techniques.

- Go directly to the source. Be direct and specific.
- Let the person know what you find acceptable and unacceptable behavior.
- Ask anyone who needs to blast off at you to please do so in private.
- Remember that all people deserve your respect, even if you don't like how they are acting.
- Don't judge or blame; it wastes time and distracts you from the task at hand.
- Accept that you can try to change others, but you can't make them change.
- Look at the root of the problem, not just the symptoms.
- Stay neutral by saying something like "Oh?" or "Really?"
- Be direct and specific in a tactful manner.
- Maintain calm persistence.
- Keep control of your own emotions.

Be a Dynamic Business Liaison

Liaison means connecting link. You're a connecting link. Think of all the people you connect your manager(s) to and with. You are an integral player as a contact between your manager(s) and the organization and the rest of the world. This is an important role and position. You must view it as one of high importance and learn the techniques that will make you a dynamic connector of people.

Be at Least as Good as Your Manager, if Not Better

In other words, you should be as educated, talented and professional-looking in your own area of expertise as your manager is in his or hers. There may be areas where you even surpass your manager, such as business protocol or proper etiquette. This attitude is especially important if you want to move up the career ladder.

Use Business Protocol

To use business protocol, you have to know business protocol. Since this topic lends itself to entire books, you are encouraged to patronize your local library and bookstores. There are many fine books from which to choose.

One that I referred to earlier, *Everday Business Etiquette* by Marilyn Pincus, can be ordered by visiting my Web site, www.officedynamicsltd.com. In her book, Pincus explores many topics. For example, she writes about special seating arrangements: "You may oversee a meeting with variously titled people seated on stage. Ascertain protocol before assigning seats so you don't unintentionally insult an elected official, a judge, professor, member of the armed services or some other titled attendee.

"If you do insult someone, you are not likely to be the only one who is criticized. The company you represent and your business associates may be subjected to chastisement and ridicule for this inappropriate behavior, too.

"It may be necessary to research guests' official ranks. There are numerous offices of protocol you may contact for information, as well as a dignitary's home office."

Follow Social Etiquette

Just as there is business protocol, there is social etiquette. Unfortunately, proper etiquette has fallen by the wayside, with many people today embracing a relaxed style in everything from their voice mail recordings to their failure to write thank-you notes or respond to R.S.V.P.s. *Inner circle* professionals don't do these things. They strive to display proper social etiquette.

Be Poised

Poise means walking light-footedly with your head held high, shoulders back and wearing a smile. Poise involves eating gracefully in front of others. It's the way you drink your cup of coffee and eat at a business luncheon. Poise is the icing on the cake. It's the final touch! How does one gain poise? It's hard if you have not been taught it as a child, but you can learn it. Watch others who impress you, who seem to have style and grace and know how to handle themselves. Practice. Ask a mentor to evaluate you. Do not ask a good friend. Your friends will not be as objective and may not be totally honest with you.

Make it a Way of Life

Being a superb business liaison is a way of life. It's something you learn, embrace, believe in and, therefore, use to the best of your ability every chance you get.

Know the Little Things

A savvy liaison knows the little things, like which side to wear a name tag. (By the way, it is the right side.) It's knowing when and how to interrupt someone in a meeting.

Good Office Manners Are Crucial to Business Success

"Where Have Our Manners Gone?" was the main headline of a lengthy *USA Today* article I once read. This article caught my immediate interest for two reasons:

1. In meeting people nationwide, I've noticed a decline in manners.
2. A number of our clients are asking me to focus on business etiquette in my training programs.

Good Manners is Good Business!

Good office manners are a crucial part of your career success. All business experts agree that good manners mean good business. Ann Marie Sabath, author of *Business Etiquette in Brief*, says the following:

"The world has become high-tech and complicated. Yet basic courtesies have never gone out of style. Quite the contrary. In today's business environment they become even more crucial to gaining a competitive edge. Consider the following.

"Automation has become an integral part of our lives. The more high-tech our world becomes, the more important effective interpersonal communication will be.

"Men and women have become colleagues. Each year, women continue to be promoted to management positions, not without kinks. Social rules from yesteryear are suddenly called into question.

"Many of today's young business people are part of the McManners Drive-thru Generation. Despite the fact that numerous trips to the fast food lane may not have exposed this generation to some of the table manners basic to those reared in less frenzied times, today's young professionals are still expected to possess a certain degree of finesse once they enter the business world."

Letitia Baldrige, who wrote the Foreword for *Everyday Business Etiquette*, puts it this way: "Most parents today, particularly single and dual-career parents, don't have the time to teach civility to their children the way they learned it from their parents and grandparents.

"Civility is fading away from us, and it shows up more clearly in the workplace than anywhere else (with the exception of the way people drive their cars on the freeways and on crowded city streets.) Marilyn Pincus is a fighter for civility. She knows that success in business depends as much on the human element and people skills as it does on a person's dexterity with a mouse and spreadsheets."

Good manners certainly give you the edge when someone else has the same skill level as you. If you want to make a positive first impression, think about your posture, language and overall appearance. To be highly skilled and then not display good manners will surely destroy your career in the long run.

What Are Good Manners?

As a general overall statement, Sue Fox, author of *Etiquette for Dummies*, says, "Manners are about self-respect and respecting others and making people feel comfortable." As for specifics, let me provide you with a few:

- *Punctuality!*
- *A firm handshake.*
- *Saying "please" and "thank you."*
- *Responding to an R.S.V.P. by the deadline date.*
- *Being focused when someone is speaking to you.*
- *Standing at your desk and shaking hands when introduced.*
- *Walking through the office with poise.*
- *Gracefully entering an office or a meeting room.*
- *Treating everyone with courtesy and fairness.*
- *Being impeccably groomed.*
- *Promptly returning phone calls.*
- *Chewing with your mouth closed.*
- *Recognizing cultural differences.*

As easy as it is for me to list the above, it is just as easy for me to list the things you need to avoid such as:

- *Loud laughing or talking.*
- *Crying in front of others.*
- *A messy desk with little trinkets or stuffed animals placed all over.*
- *Not keeping confidences.*
- *Barging into someone's office.*

- *Ill-mannered cell phone use such as talking loudly (this is called "cell yell") or using your cell phone in restaurants, especially where there is formal dining.*
- *Leaving your phone on in training sessions or seminars.*
- *Discussing personal business in public areas.*
- *Negative attitudes or complaining to coworkers.*
- *Aggressiveness.*

A Few Words About Introductions

Establishing rapport with others begins with the first few minutes of contact. This is when your people skills, or lack of them, will be displayed. You exude success and confidence when you smile, make eye contact and shake hands firmly.

Rules to Remember
- *Stand when welcoming someone into your office or as she approaches your desk, unless it's someone you work with all the time.*
- *Reflect a friendly facial expression — smile.*
- *Shake hands firmly. A firm handshake shows confidence, warmth and sincerity. A weak handshake indicates doubt, insecurity and apprehension.*
- *Use good eye contact.*
- *When male and female are introduced, either may initiate the handshake.*
- *When making introductions, the higher-ranking person is addressed first.*

General
- *When someone addresses you by the wrong name, just restate your name to avoid embarrassing them.*
- *When you forget someone's name, welcome the person with a handshake and reintroduce yourself. Most of the time, they will respond positively.*

- *If you are unsure how to address a woman, use Ms.*

You might think these ideas are simplistic, ones that all people know. Yet it is amazing to me, in my consulting and training business, how many people I come in contact with who don't make proper introductions and use common courtesy.

When You Feel as Though It's Toooo Much!

Take a close look at what you think is important and must be done today. When my mother died and I was out of town for a full week, I learned a good lesson. The things that I thought were so important and had to get done waited. And you know what? Some weren't even missed by others. Start determining the things, events, people that are most important to you, and stop getting caught up in things that really don't matter. Enjoy your life more! Laugh more! Spend more time with your kids, parents, sisters and brothers. Take a walk in the rain. Watch a sunset. Look at a full moon. Pay attention to the beauty of each season. And take time to learn the rules and to be courteous to everyone with whom you interact each day.

Are You a Good Office Concierge?

In numerous surveys conducted by Office Dynamics, Ltd., managers have stated that they want their administrative assistant to be an excellent business liaison. As I mentioned earlier, you connect your manager to many people inside and outside the organization. Here, I would like to focus on your role as a connector with outsiders, particularly visitors from other cities or countries.

When someone is visiting a company for the first time in a strange city, he usually looks to the administrative assistant to recommend hotels, restaurants and limo services. He relies on the assistant to let him know where to go in town as well as any unsafe areas. If his stay is long, he expects you to know what may be

185

going on in your town culturally—the arts and music. He may be sports fans.

Since these city foreigners rely on you, you shouldn't recommend anything that you have not personally checked or heard accolades about from a close colleague or your boss. I have had situations where administrative assistants recommended hotels in which the rooms were old and needed repair. Or they sent me to restaurants that they had heard about but never dined at personally, where the food wasn't that great and the service was poor.

So, set a goal of being an excellent concierge. Test caterers before you recommend them. See a hotel room, not the just the lobby. Eat at different restaurants. Find out who has the best limo service in town, even if you don't travel by limo. Collect brochures and newspaper articles that focus on events in your city, the arts, music, and theater. You will truly shine to that visitor and leave a positive long-lasting impression.

Stay on the Cutting Edge

Inner circle achievers have several strategies for staying on the cutting edge. Of course, one of the best ways is to sharpen your mind regularly. If you want to learn something new, brush up on your skills or earn a degree. The Web is making it easier to further your education. Here are some tips on getting started.

1. Check out your options. Online courses vary in what they offer. Some are free; others require a fee. Some offer traditional degrees; others provide certification.

2. Go to online catalogs. Search by subject or location to get information on fees, courses offered and contacts. One recommended site: Teaching & Learning at www.mcli.dist.maricopa.edu/tl/index.html.

3. Try the demos. Several colleges and universities provide online demos of how courses are conducted online. A recommended site: Wisconsin Technical

College System at consortiurn.tec.wi.us/demos.
The site provides a collection of demos.

4. Check out non-university sites. There are other organizations that provide workplace training programs online. Many focus on computer/technical training. Recommended sites:

  - DigitalThink at www.digitalthink.com.
  - Ziff Davis Network at www.zdu.com.

Spotlighting Professional Image

Much of what has been discussed, in this chapter in particular, has an impact on your professional image. Your command (or lack of command) of business etiquette is an excellent example. What is the first word or words that come to your mind when you hear or read "professional image"? If you are like most of the thousands of administrative professionals I've asked that question to over the years, your answers will be "appearance" or "dress." Then you might think of body language, actions, speech and other aspects of appearance, such as how one stands or walks. It's important to put the spotlight on the topic now, because the *inner circle* assistant must be completely conversant with the phenomenon.

I define professional image as the culmination of your demeanor, your manner of speech and your appearance. It also encompasses:

- *respect*
- *personal identity*
- *harmony*
- *self-confidence*
- *attitude*
- *self-esteem*
- *teamwork*
- *professional knowledge*

Inner circle assistants use every situation to present a powerful professional image; they know another opportunity may not come along. While I will not delve into the details of professional image in terms of appearance and dress (because there are excellent resources available in this area), it is very important that you are aware of its impact on your success. I encourage you to purchase a book or two by image experts. In fact, we carry an excellent book called *Casual Power* by Sherry Monsonave. It is one of the best resources I have found that details the six levels of casual dress. (Call our office at 800-STAR-139 for more information.)

Now I would like to address why it is important to reflect a professional image.

- ***You are a representative of your organization.*** *While your company may embrace casual dress, there are six levels of casual dress. Does your company want its employees to follow business casual or sporty casual? While you are your own being from 8:00 a.m. to 5:00 p.m., you are still representing your company. This is especially important if you meet with vendors, outsiders, community professionals or clients. On the other hand, don't think it doesn't apply to you if you sit in the back office and rarely interact with outsiders.*

- ***You are your own calling card.*** *According to Susan Bixler, author of* The New Professional Image, *it only takes 30 seconds for people to form numerous impressions about you, such as your education level, career competence, personality, level of sophistication, trustworthiness, skills, talent and social heritage. Susan also talks about the halo effect. She says, "These quick impressions can be lasting ones. When your visual message is positive, the person you've just met will tend to assume that other aspects about you are equally positive. But unfortunately, if your visual message is negative, that* *new customer, client, coworker or prospective employer may not spend the time and effort to discover the talented person inside."*

- **People take you more seriously.** *You might say professional image is about perception. If people perceive you to be frivolous because of the outfit you are wearing, then that is the reality they live with. When you look like you are serious about going to work, people take you more seriously. If you find that people or managers are not taking your opinion to heart, not including you in making decisions or not giving you those meaty assignments, you may want to take a close look at your choice of dress for the office.*

- **You inspire others!** *Yes, when you look like you spent time and gave thought to what you selected to wear for the day, you inspire those around you. Years ago, when I was working as an executive assistant for Steelcase, Inc. in North Carolina, an outside visitor who came in to see my executive complimented me on how nice I looked and said it made him feel good to see me looking so nice. You also can inspire others to improve their overall image. The inner circle assistant is a leader when it comes to dress and appearance.*

There is one myth I feel I must address, and it has to do with money. Often, when I speak on professional image and especially dress, I hear participants say, "If my company paid me more, I would look better." It has nothing to do with money! It has everything to do with how you pull your look together, clothing that fits your body shape, neatly pressed clothes and wearing colors that enhance your natural beauty. I hate to date myself, but when I started working in offices in 1970, I only made about $7,000.00 per year! But I always looked nice. If you are going to spend money on clothes, you may as well select the clothing that makes you look your personal best! Occasionally, you may want to invest in one or two nicer pieces. The good part of investing in a higher quality item of clothing is that it lasts longer, so it really isn't as expensive as you think. For example, if you purchase a very nice classic-looking blazer or jacket for $180 and can wear if for five years (because of the quality), it only costs you $36 per year. The world is ever-changing when it comes to dress, image and appearance. Remember that this includes your hair, eyeglasses, shoes, jewelry, hose and even your handbag or briefcase. The *inner circle* assistant keeps herself or himself abreast of the latest business trends in these areas. Invest in some good books, look up image experts on the Internet and even meet with an image expert in your community. It will be time well spent.

Then & Now — A Looking-Glass View

Then: Professional demeanor was dictated by society at large. The support person labored primarily in the office environment and didn't assume an authority role.

Now: You're on stage all the time. You're being watched by visitors. The way you look, speak and act adds or detracts from your credibility. You live and breathe with the Perception Factor. If others perceive you to be professional, they will deal with you accordingly. You work all the time to boost this image and keep it up on a pedestal. It has everything to do with the respect you'll receive and the goals you'll achieve.

The *inner circle* professional may be casually dressed, but she doesn't look as though she's going to the beach. Strange as it may seem to some folks, power is heavily rooted in appearance. Even when her boss and her company approve of casual dress, the *inner circle* professional realizes the boss may not really mean it. Or his version of casual dress may mean that a blazer be worn along with those carefully pressed linen pants and that casual silk blouse.

COMPETENCY 9

Professional Development

"Without goals, and plans to reach them, you are like a ship that has set sail with no destination," wrote Fitzhugh Dodson, a one-time high school teacher who later became a child psychologist.

"First you write down your goal; your second job is to break down your goal into a series of steps, beginning with steps that are absurdly easy." This is another Dodson observation.

Since he moved from being a teacher to a psychologist and author, we can safely assume Fitzhugh Dodson practiced what he preached!

How About You?

Your future at work depends on one thing—taking charge of your own career. As time marches on, jobs as we once knew them have been transformed. In some companies, there are no titles, no corner offices and no clear hierarchy. You are required to be not only an individual contributor but a team member and innovator. Once you recognize you can choose your destination and then takes steps to get there, life is not boring! Here are some tips to help you become truly indispensable.

- *Think like an entrepreneur. See yourself as the president of You, Inc. Don't just think of yourself as working for someone else; learn to take responsibility and be accountable for your work environment. Quit waiting for management to create the culture. Be a catalyst in making good things happen where you work.*

- *Think "teams." See beyond you and your manager as a team. Think of your department colleagues as your teammates. See people in other departments as part of the bigger team. A company should be a constellation of talent. As each person becomes better at what he or she does and shares successes with the others, each department becomes stronger. As each department becomes more effective, the entire organization excels.*

- *Be a problem solver. Long gone are the days of running to management with problems and letting them solve them. In the new work environment, you will have to tackle problems inside and outside your immediate area. When you see a problem, take ownership. Think of several solutions, evaluate possible outcomes, select one and more forward.*

- *Take risks. Taking risks can be scary. When you take a risk, you usually are not guaranteed of the outcome. But if you never take a risk — push your limits — you will never know your true potential.*

- *Seek feedback. All of us have blind spots. While we may think we know all our strengths and weaknesses, others see us in a different light. Encourage feedback from your manager, colleagues, customers and others who interact with you regularly. Once you receive their feedback, work on a plan for improvement.*

President of Your Career

Regardless of your career goal, make yourself president of your career. You will…

- *Transform yourself to stay competitive.*

- *Think of yourself as working for yourself, not just a department or another person.*
- *Think of yourself as an independent contractor with a bag of top-notch skills.*

Think of a name for your company (you) and fill in the blanks below. List as many assets (e.g., strengths, skills, attitudes) as you can. Be sure to list your liabilities, too (areas for growth, skills needed to be learned, attitudes you need to embrace). *If you don't want to write in the book, you're at liberty to copy this page.*

Company name _____

Today's Date _____

Assets	Liabilities

What will you do to transform your liabilities into assets?

_____

_____

_____

Follow-up:

From time to time, review the list you generated. Are your liabilities being transformed so they eventually become assets? As that happens, and it should, list new liabilities to work on.

Organizations must also be aware of their competition.
1. Who is your competition?
2. What can you do to gain a competitive advantage?

You don't necessarily have to be in competition with other people; you can be your own challenger. How? It's easy. Compete against yourself to be better than you are today. Look for little ways to consistently evaluate what you're doing and thinking. *Set goals. Break down goals into a series of steps, beginning with steps which are absurdly easy.*

Illustration

A soft speaking voice doesn't sound authoritative and can be one reason your suggestions go unnoticed. Since wishing won't transform your speaking voice, join a weekly speaker's group (e.g., a local Toastmaster's International club), participate in the church choir or work with a voice coach. You can even do all three. (It's absurdly easy!)

Attitude - Keep Your Positive Focus

Remember: The most important attribute of a successful person is attitude with a positive slant. Here is a list of ways to keep your mind focused on the positive side of every event. Post this list next to your desk, in your car, at home by the mirror and, if necessary, inside your laptop case.

- *Laugh in the face of adversity.*
- *Get excited by every achievement, no matter how small.*
- *Never dwell on misfortunes; they're mental depressants.*
- *Associate with people who have a positive outlook.*
- *Treat each experience as another step toward realizing your dreams.*
- *Commitment, action and self-esteem determine your outcomes.*
- *Consistency is not a luxury; it's a necessity!*

Land the Job You Really Want Without Leaving the Company

It's the perfect time to create a new job or reinvent the one you have now. And all this may be possible without leaving the company. Mergers, acquisitions, buyouts and other modern-day realities impact business. Therefore, the climate is likely to be ripe for your personal career growth and can result in a boon for your company.

It's not easy to create a new job, but the key is to match your talents and aspirations with your company's needs. Here are three early steps to take toward your dream job:

- *Start by asking yourself what you do really well and how you can get to do more of it.*
- *Don't wait to get permission. (See comments on Expansion below.) If you want to incorporate more responsibility into your position, no manager will argue — especially if you can do it successfully.*
- *Seek feedback. All of us have blind spots. While we may think we know all our strengths and weaknesses, others see us in a different light. Encourage feedback from your manager, colleagues, customers, and others who interact with you regularly. Once you receive their feedback, work on a plan for improvement. (Remember, absurdly easy steps aren't as threatening and, therefore, get you going.)*

As these actions move you closer to your goal, you'll discover other actions that seem appropriate. Act on them, too.

Expansion — A Key Building Block

- *Take advantage of opportunities to learn more and apply what you learn here and now!*
- *Volunteer for teams, job rotation or job sharing. Do not wait to be asked. Look for opportunities to get involved.*
- *Delegate your work to others to free up time to work on new initiatives.*
- *Volunteer to take the lead on key projects that will increase your visibility.*

- *Look for opportunities to sit in on meetings, ask questions and express opinions.*

Gossip: A Career Management Tool

Not all gossip is bad. In fact, the grapevine can be a valuable source of information to help you in your career. Consider that some gossip can be intentional leaks of information you should know or that the grapevine can help you cultivate sources of information. Here is how to make the grapevine work for you:

Listen actively.

There's no need to comment on anything. But if you keep an *ear open*, you may pick up information that could help you, like expected layoffs or an opening in another department.

Don't send out a holier-than-thou message.

If people perceive that you consider gossip beneath you, they'll cut you out. Not that you should fuel the flame of negative gossip. Learn to distinguish between energy that is wasted on useless hearsay and helpful *grapevine* communication.

Don't add grist to the mill.

Don't feel so pressed to contribute to the exchange that you say something that could come back to haunt you.

Respond carefully.

Even a harmless nod of agreement could be misinterpreted. Think before you speak. Choose your words carefully. You may even ask the other person to repeat what she thought you said/how you responded.

Create Your Own Personnel File

Since you are president of your career, you need to keep your own personnel file. Building this file gives you easy access to items you might want to share with your current boss or a new employer. Here are a few items to include:

1. Positions you have held in and out of the company (e.g., scout leader).
2. Copies of job descriptions/job analysis.
3. Performance review and/or appraisals.
4. Letters of appreciation from clients, vendors, etc.
5. Continuing-education certificates.
6. Reference letters from previous employers or managers you worked with/for.
7. Personal and workplace references, complete with contact information.
8. Samples of projects you have worked on or documents you created; use before and after samples.

Don't Feel Guilty — You Are Worth It

In one respect, it's admirable that administrative staff don't want to leave their work areas to attend training sessions because they want to be available to the people they support. As you become better educated and more skilled and develop new work habits, you better assist your team. In reality, however, you cheat the people you support when you don't learn the latest trends, upgrade your skills and reinforce fundamental administrative concepts. So put away the guilt! Get yourself to classes, seminars, workshops and on-site training. You shouldn't feel punished or guilty because you want to learn.

Get People to Notice You:

Promote yourself   *Don't let any positive accomplishment go unnoticed.*

Be visible to the right people. Determine who should know your talents. Create an assignment that will bring you into close contact with the people who can help you move ahead.

Impress people

Be a person of action. Don't worry about impressing people with words; that's the ego speaking. Impress people by doing something important or relevant. Be known as someone who comes up with ideas and gets things done.

Do something for others first. You can make a great impression by first providing a service, doing a good deed or promoting others. Think about what you can do for them. Eventually, they will be doing things for you. Can you send them information about something they are interested in? A project they are working on? Do you need to promote them to someone else? Can you tell others about these people and their product or service?

Be yourself. Impress people with who you are. Don't try to be what you think they want you to be. Let your good qualities and positive personality shine. Always speak optimistically with people. Nobody enjoys spending time with a pessimist.

Find the link. As you get to know people, think of how you connect with them. What do you have in common? Is there anything that links you together?

Build Alliances   *Get to know everyone.* Why? Because you don't know today what your needs will be a year or three years from now. You don't really know what you will be doing, where you will be working or what you'll want to achieve personally. Make an ally of every person you meet. Build an invisible Rolodex and expand your friendships. Once you have an ally and nurture that relationship, you will always have that person available to you. You never know how someone you meet today can influence your career or help you in the future.

Expand Your Network

- *Consider all the people you know today. Whom do they mention that you should get to know?*
- *Introduce yourself at every business or social function.*
- *Broaden your social circle. Make new friends. Don't stay with the same old crowd.*
- *Join several associations or professional organizations.*
- *Volunteer for community or charity work.*
- *Meet people at church.*
- *Meet your children's friends' parents; learn about what they do and where they work.*
- *Make it a monthly goal to add three acquaintances to your network.*
- *Consider your clients and suppliers. Should you strengthen lines of communication with them?*
- *Stay in contact with former bosses and coworkers.*
- *Meet people who differ from you in background and experience and become familiar with their ideas and performances.*

> "Keep company with those who make you better" is an old British saying that's well worth noting.

Pay Special Attention to Business Networks

Closely examine the position to which you aspire.

- *Dress and act as if you were already in that position.*
- *Keep yourself visible at all times.*
- *Involve yourself in a variety of activities at work, inside and outside your division.*
- *Be known as an action person.*
- *Create support networks of contacts and resources.*
- *Know the decision makers in your organization. Let them know you, and make them aware of your talents.*
- *Keep your eyes open for a position you might desire within your organization, and be ready to ask for it in the event it opens up.*
- *Strive to achieve the qualities of star performers.*
- Always *do the best you can. Leave a good track record behind you.*
- *Always leave a company accentuating the good feelings toward those you worked with and trying to eliminate the negative ones.*
- *Build quality relationships.*
- *Take people you admire to lunch. Not only are you likely to build good will, you'll have the opportunity to see how an individual behaves in a relaxed business setting. And you may pick up helpful pointers.*

Contacts Count

"It's not what you know, it's who you know." You probably have heard this statement hundreds of times. It is true, to a point. Who you know does matter. Of course, once you get past the "who," you'd better know the "what."

IMAGINE THAT a coworker tells you she's going to post for a job in the actuarial department. "I know the director of the division," she claims. "He plays golf with my dad, and they went to college together." You wish her well, but you saw the posting and noticed that it requires someone who earned a college degree with a major in business administration. Your coworker majored in history. Much to your surprise, she gets the job! You later learn that it's a temporary placement, with the provision that she return to college and earns credits in business administration. You think to yourself, "This is a who-you-know foot in the door," but you can't argue with the fairness of it. She's willing to do what it takes to satisfy needs.

Making contacts and building relationships can speed up the journey toward your goal, multiply your resources, add balance to your style and thinking and help promote you in ways you cannot possibly promote yourself. You need people to help you get where you want to go in life. You cannot do it alone.

In a Nutshell

Contacts count because they:
- *Provide guidance and support.*
- *Add to your knowledge base.*
- *Know other people you should know and can either make you aware of those people or set up introductions for you.*
- *May influence a decision that will affect your career or goal.*

Networking Smarts

Most of us have attended a number of professional, social and business events. But do you do more than hand out your business card and collect the ones handed to you? Make optimal use of these social power meetings by following these helpful tips.
- *Identify the people or person you actually would like to meet and talk with before the event. This helps you focus on a purpose and avoid fruitless card collection.*
- *Don't underestimate the power of small talk. Small talk can lead to bigger things. Don't dismiss gatherings because you rarely get past*

the chitchat. Take the opportunity to lead small talk into more meaningful and valuable exchanges.

- *Go in with an agenda. Ask yourself what you really want to get out of going to these networking sessions. Then ask yourself what you can give someone else. Conversely, when someone asks for your input, be aware of what you can provide them.*
- *Introduce yourself in a memorable way. The first thing you tell someone about yourself should capture her or his attention.*
- *Reconnect after the meeting. Don't just exchange business cards. Set a specific time and day to meet again, either in person or with a phone call. Do it within the first week of the event.*

Your Body — An Important Corporate Asset?

You bet! Most of us are so busy, we often neglect our most important valuable asset — our own bodies. We think we can't take time for ourselves, as that is selfish. We talk ourselves into believing that going to the gym is something we do only to lose weight, to look better. Many people, especially administrative staff, don't think they have time to take a lunch break, because they have to get their work done. Don't neglect fine-tuning your health. There's plenty of instructional literature and advice available. Plug it in and see for yourself if it makes a positive difference. *Eating breakfast* is one of my favorites. You can't shake my acceptance of this rule. I learned a long time ago that breakfast helps keep my corporate self humming along efficiently until midday.

Stay Competitive

Nobody can afford to rest on a reputation anymore. Circumstances change too quickly. Competition gets tougher and more global all the time. What we consider "good" today is seen as "so-so" by tomorrow. Every single employee should assume personal responsibility for upgrading his or her job performance.

— Price Pritchett

Training

Take advantage of every vehicle available to you: workshops, seminars, books, audio and video tapes or Internet. Don't overlook any tool (product or person) that you can learn from.

Retraining

Brush up on old skills. It never hurts to reinforce or confirm what you already know. New ways of doing old things are continually being developed, and you need to stay on top of them.

Kaizen

Kaizen is the Japanese term for continuous improvement. Continuously improve. Don't be satisfied with where you are today; you can do better. You can stretch outside your comfort zone and go to the next level.

Marketing

You market yourself all the time. Keep yourself *sharp* and come across as professional and knowledgeable. Demonstrate that you're flexible and mobile.

Listening

Listen for new ideas and opportunities. If you don't need them today, you may need them in the future.

Assemble a Bag of Topnotch Skills

Consistently assemble a bag of topnotch skills. Instead of dismissing a skill that isn't needed for the work you perform today, think about the future. You never know when your job will change and require new skills and attitudes. There is no guarantee you will have the job you have today even six months from now. Don't wait and be caught off guard. Time may not permit you to attain expert, status, but do expose yourself to all kinds of skills as you go along. Then, if you need to perfect any of them, you'll have a head start.

Criticism Can Hurt

Sometimes it hurts when we are criticized, especially when we think we've done a good job or handled a situation the best we could. Many people take criticism about their work personally. They carry it with them all day and bring it home to their families. When this happens, their work is affected, their attitude toward coworkers and customers is affected, and they make costly mistakes.

Looking for the Lesson

If you find it difficult to accept criticism, you might be focusing too much on extraneous factors. These are things people let get in the way, so they never really hear the message the sender is trying to send. Some of these factors include:

Type of criticism	Vicious
	Jealous
Who is criticizing	Someone we dislike
	A superior
Tone of voice	Sarcastic
	Condescending

Not all people know how to give or accept criticism. Most of us have not taken Criticism 101 in school! But criticism can be a learning experience if you view it positively.

When being criticized about your work performance:

Disregard	Body language
	Tone of voice
	Facial expression
Focus on	The context of what is being said
Ask yourself	Could this person be right?
	Should I have handled that situation differently?
	What can I learn from what this person is telling me?

For example, if your manager is being critical of your work or attitude, take a step back and think to yourself that maybe he or she is right. Maybe you could do better, change a habit or improve your performance. It's easy to take criticism personally, but try to view the situation objectively and see how things may look from your manager's perspective.

Accepting Criticism

Inner circle performers accept criticism and use it to their advantage.

Think in terms of criticism as a possible gift. (Take a moment to peel away the wrapper and examine the contents.)

- *Let defensive feelings go.*
- *Don't take the criticism personally.*
- *Disregard facial expression and tone of voice.*
- *Look for the lesson.*

Professional Development — Career Portfolio

Whether you decide you want to move up in your chosen field, move out of the profession or stay where you are, a career portfolio will be a valuable asset to you.

Why would it be beneficial to create a career portfolio?

- *Shows you are proactive.*
- *You'd have a hard copy — a permanent history — of your accomplishments.*
- *Shows people what you're capable of doing.*
- *A tool to receive higher levels of recognition.*
- *Shows your creativity.*

When and where can you use it?

- *During your performance review.*
- *When writing your professional development plan for the upcoming year and tracking accomplishments.*
- *Competing for an internal job.*
- *When a new boss comes on board and you want him or her to quickly gain an overview of your talents and experiences.*
- *Asking for additional responsibility.*
- *Outside work, if you are trying to obtain a leadership role.*
- *When being considered for committee work.*
- *External interviewing.*

What can you put into this portfolio? Many things, but here are some suggestions:

- *Professional photo of yourself (no larger than 4 x 6).*
- *Record of any outside work such as volunteer or committee work.*
- *Thank-you notes from customers or clients on a job well done.*
- *Thank-you letters from other divisions or executives on a job well done.*
- *Examples of your work: graphic work, spreadsheets, etc. (Be careful you do not divulge confidential company information).*
- *Past evaluations (not more than three years old).*
- *Your mission statement and vision.*
- *Customer appreciation letters.*
- *Resume (Have extra copies in the back pocket if you use a three-ring binder).*
- *Personal profilers.*

- *Emphasize results and accomplishments vs. job duties!*

Be sure to place this in a nice leather portfolio, possibly with your initials on it. Or you might want to use a three-ring binder. Be creative. Remember the outside packaging also represents you and will send a message to the person viewing your portfolio. Strive for clean lines, a professional look and quality products. Also think about the font style and size you will use as well as the type and color paper; again, keep it professional. You might want to use some nice sheet protectors as well. Extras could include a table of contents, cover letter and an informational CD!

Note: You do not leave this portfolio with the interviewer or others reviewing it. That is why you might want to leave an informational CD and have extra copies of your resume on hand.

Then & Now — A Looking-Glass View

Then: The assistant may have attended a feel-good seminar once a year as a reward. She or he didn't map out development goals.

Now: The *inner circle* professional must identify goals that need development in the upcoming year. The goals must mesh with the executive's goals as well as department and organization goals. *Accountability* is the operating word. She will be tracked by management during the year to see how well she's doing to meet those goals. She's getting more intense training, and as good as she is today, she realizes she has many, many areas in which she has to grow.

COMPETENCY 10

Supporting Multiple Managers

Managing Multiple Managers

While administrative professionals today typically support between four and six people, some assistants manage up to 35 people. They support these individuals with everything from computer work to assistance on major projects. This trend is likely to continue into the 21st century. As overwhelming as this might seem, today's professional can direct the flow of work and gain a sense of control by using creative methods.

Activity: Complete the following by indicating your feelings with a check mark.

	AGREE	DISAGREE
The first person to bring me his work gets his work done first.		
It is impossible to support more than six people.		
First, complete work for the people you like the most.		
Let the managers fight it out as to whose work should get done first.		
Everything will take care of itself, if given enough time.		
I am an integral player in coordinating projects, tasks and people.		

SCORE: The information that follows reveals whether experts agree with your choices.

Tips for Managing Multiple Managers

- *Except for time-critical projects, do the senior manager's work first.*
- *If your managers are on the same level, complete the task with the earliest due date first.*
- *Find out what projects are coming up so you can plan accordingly.*
- *Ask your managers to give you project materials as sections are ready. This will help prevent a last-minute rush.*
- *Communicate! Stay informed, and keep your managers informed.*

Five Ways to a Guilt-Free No

Let's face it; some of us really have trouble saying no. So before you take on yet another project, examine whether or not you truly can contribute your best to it. If you find that you can't, try these ways to say an unapologetic no. (This list isn't a reason to not tell the truth, but it helps you to word what you need to say in a more effective manner.)

- *"Several unexpected things happened at work or home, and it would be best if I dealt with them first before I took on more."*
- *"I've had some experience with that work, and I didn't contribute as well as I should have. Maybe it would be better if I didn't participate this time."*
- *"I really have a lot of faith and confidence in you. I'm sure you'll do an excellent job."*
- *"I know I don't do very well when my mind and time are so divided. I just don't feel confident that I'll be able to give my best at this time."*
- *"I'm truly striving for excellence, and taking on too many projects makes me more mediocre and less focused than I'd like to be."*

Juggling—It's Not Just for Circus Performers!

Today, many office professionals are supporting multiple people. Here are some sure-fire strategies for keeping things flowing smoothly and reducing workplace stress.

1. Encourage managers to use uniform procedures. It really helps keep things simpler when everyone uses similar procedures.
2. Limit personal jobs for managers. Learn to say no (e.g., discussed above).
3. Treat each manager fairly and with respect, despite your personal preference. You may not like everyone you support, but you do need to treat each person equally.
4. Understand each manager's unique work style. While you may encourage uniform procedures, do pay attention to the work style that best suits each manager.

5. Establish a priority list for all to see and update it frequently. Either post this in a common area for all to see or distribute weekly. This allows all the managers to be aware of what and how many projects you are involved in, and it helps them understand why their work isn't turned around in a day.
6. Communicate regularly with all your managers. Be sure to inform them of any delays.

Increasing Team Productivity

The organization in which you work should not just be viewed as "the employer." Organizations are contexts in which you can learn and grow; they are groups of experienced people who are willing to pass their knowledge on to you, to demonstrate their skills so you can improve yours and to give you an opportunity to try your wings in an environment that no one person could create.
— Margaret Higgenson & Thomas Quick
The Ambitious Woman's Guide to a Successful Career

Groups of people may be thrown together due to circumstances, work environment or titles, but that doesn't mean they will successfully thrive. Star-performing teams take time to develop into a vibrant force in an organization. It takes a plan, desire, time and hard work to mesh into a unit of one.

- *Set specific attainable goals.*
- *Have a plan.*
- *Set priorities.*
- *Anticipate obstacles and how to get around them.*
- *Ensure that all team members are committed to the goals and know the team's mission.*
- *Communicate, communicate.*

- *Learn your teammates' habits and peculiarities. Accept them. Look for their strengths and good qualities.*
- *Be creative.*
- *Assess the abilities of each team player. Identify strengths and assign tasks or responsibilities based on each person's talents.*
- *Attend training sessions and encourage other team players to attend training.*

Then & Now — A Looking-Glass View

Then: It wasn't necessary to support multiple managers.

Now: It's commonplace. One of the reasons for this is the advent of technology and the belief that one *inner circle* professional can do a good job of supporting multiple managers. Communication excellence is of paramount importance. It's necessary to routinely update all those *personalities* and make sure you obtain the information you need from them to stay on task. It is a juggling act — no doubt about it. But, much like a juggler who basks in the glow of the roar of the crowd — when you get accolades for a job well done, you're in the big tent!

COMPETENCY 11

Task & Project Management

It's simple; tasks are ongoing activities that are usually a part of everyday work. Projects have defined starting points and deadline dates. That's the only part that's simple! Getting from point A to point Z takes some maneuvering, and that's what the *inner circle* assistant makes look as though it's simple!

Keeping Project Work Flowing

List the types of projects you work on and their frequency (daily, weekly, monthly, quarterly).

PROJECT
_____

_____

_____

FREQUENCY
_____

_____

_____

NOTES/PROCESS
_____

_____

_____

Tips

- *Use expandable pocket folders.*

- o Different sizes
- o Different colors
- o Closed with clasps or open tops
- *Use your follow-up system to be informed about what to expect next.*
- *Take advantage of software programs.*
- *Use wall charts.*
- *Create a calendar overview — one month only — to capture each important step and display it on the appropriate date. All parties involved should get a copy of this calendar. You might add a more detailed sheet to the calendar.*
- *Create a current projects list and update it regularly. If feasible, hang a chart on a wall where all concerned parties can view it. Include deadlines, milestones and projects on hold. Route a copy to those who consistently funnel work your way. It helps them determine your availability.*

Key Concepts

1. Make sure all parties involved in the project get a copy.
2. Update *all* of the systems you're using (calendar, software program, etc.), regularly.
3. Keep all parties involved in the project informed as changes occur, tasks get accomplished, dates change, etc.
4. Do status updates regularly.
5. Anticipate upcoming projects.
6. Map out an estimated plan.
7. Delegate when possible.
8. Have all your resources and materials ready when you start.

One Word

If you were asked to sum up all of the above in one word, would you agree that *communication* would be the word? Task and project management generally involves two or more people. Assuming there are many components related to tasks and projects, it would be impossible to work together to reach a common goal unless you were communicating. If you're managing a task or a project alone, you still have to *track* timelines, specific activities and expectations. When you chart, document or make notes for yourself, you're communicating with yourself!

Taking Critical Feedback

The *inner circle* assistant will expect critical feedback to be delivered anywhere at any time. It's reasonable to discuss it in this chapter since task & project management is usually a work in progress. Rarely does anything occur the same way twice! Critical feedback actually works to your advantage, because it alerts you to bumps in the road and permits you to get things back on track in a timely manner.

As you request and receive feedback from coworkers and managers, you want to develop the skill of accepting feedback. Most people don't like to be told they're less than perfect. You're probably in that number. While some people aren't the best at offering constructive criticism, you may still benefit from it. Here are some techniques to help you:

- *Try to schedule face-to-face meetings with your manager. Some managers dislike providing critical feedback one on one, so they end up writing criticisms on paper or e-mail. This just raises tensions. If your manager operates this way, let him or her know that you prefer to discuss these things face to face.*
- *If you're the victim of public humiliation, calmly take aside the person who is criticizing you. Tell that person you would like to know how you can improve but would rather keep these discussions between the two of you.*
- *Don't become defensive, argumentative or angry. Instead, ask how you can specifically do things differently. And take notes.*

- *If you disagree with the feedback, simply change the perceptions. Criticism allows you to know how you are being perceived. So if the perception is wrong, don't get angry; change it! At the same time, don't neglect to be assertive if you firmly believe that your way is the right way to continue. You may need a time out to gather facts and figures that support your claims. Keep your focus on facts and outcomes, and don't stray onto the topic of personalities. You may privately think that someone is inept, etc., but it rarely does anything to advance your position if you share this information. As a matter of fact, it can cause you grief.*
- *Act on the information. Let your supervisor know about your attempts to improve. This way you can demonstrate that you're sincere about improving your work.*

Then & Now — A Looking-Glass View

Then: People always had to prioritize, follow directions and keep the lines of communication open. But the support person didn't think in terms of that would benefit the company.

Now: You have to be *outstanding* at your tasks. We're working at a faster pace, and information is coming at us from many sources (e.g., e-mail, voice mail, ground mail), and many different kinds of people (i.e., cultures) are working with you. As a result, different approaches to the same challenges are not unusual. Frequently, the *inner circle* assistant initiates projects, and troubleshooting comes with the territory. In times gone by, troubleshooting was not in the support person's job description!

COMPETENCY 12

Time Management

Time

Nothing is longer, since it is the measure of eternity.
Nothing is shorter, since it is insufficient for the
accomplishment of our projects.
Nothing is more slow to him that expects; nothing
more rapid to him that enjoys.
In greatness, it extends to infinity; in smallness,
it is infinitely divisible.
All men neglect it; all regret the loss of it; nothing can
be done without it.
It consigns to oblivion whatever is unworthy of being
transmitted to posterity, and it immortalizes
such actions as are truly great.

- Zadig

This observation is pleasing to ponder, but this chapter is filled with use-them-now tips and suggestions that can assist you in managing time (or, as some remind us, managing life around us so that time is used well). Feel free to examine this chapter anytime you feel that you've got too much to do and too little time in which to do it! A quick refresher of time-tested principles should work wonders!

Get Help Without Sounding Whiny

You're swamped, and you desperately need help getting things done. How do you get the help you need without sounding like you have dropped the ball? Here are some suggestions:

1. Arrange a 15-minute meeting with your manager. Tell her you want some feedback on a project. Remember, though, the tone of your voice and how you present the information is important. You want to come across professionally and from a perspective of valuing her input.

2. Write down your responsibilities and how much time those take. When writing the amount of time it takes, quantify it in terms of how much time it takes to do it right versus doing it in a rush.

3. Try to prioritize your list before asking for your manager's help. You determine which you think is the most important, based on what you know. You will want to bring this list to the meeting.

4. Start the conversation on a positive note, saying how excited you are about the project. Share your list, explaining how you developed the order of priority. Be open-minded, and if your manager gives her view at that time, listen.

5. If your manager has not given any input initially because she was listening and absorbing what you said, then ask for her input when you have finished presenting your information.

6. Continue to make suggestions and ask questions for clarification.

7. During your conversation, do not discuss why you haven't gotten further on the project or task. You will sound like you are just making excuses.

From Chaos to Control — A Checklist

- *Remember that, flexibility leads to control.*
- *Use your to-do list or other tools, but don't let those tools control you.*
- *Avoid backlogs of work; keep up regularly.*
- *Prioritize, prioritize.*
- *Streamline your job. Simplify for increased efficiency.*
- *Focus on the task at hand to accomplish more work in less time.*
- *Eliminate unnecessary chores.*
- *Anticipate upcoming work, events or projects.*
- *Be prepared for disasters.*
- *Know your computer. Take advantage of all it can do.*
- *Don't confuse busyness with productivity.*

Cope With Conflicting Priorities

What do you do? Every person who brings you an assignment or gives you a task to perform says it's important or tells you it's needed right away. Below are some general guidelines. Use the ones that best fit your situation.

- *Ask for specific deadlines — not ASAP.*
- *Use the FIFO (first in, first out) system.*
- *Ask the group to decide the order of priorities and then tell you.*
- *Clarify early in the day the most important priority for that day.*
- *Do the work first for the person who gives your performance evaluation.*
- *Make deadlines public information.*

- *Start a log sheet.*
- *Make your own decision and stand by it.*
- *Have the people you support complete a work-request form, establishing deadline date and time the work was submitted.*
- *Make a to-do list and estimate time for each item.*

The ABCs of Prioritizing

Prioritize your tasks according to the following system:

A	This item is of extreme importance.
B	This item is important, but could wait until tomorrow if absolutely necessary.
C	Not necessary to complete today.

Steps for categorizing:

1. Place tasks into an A, B or C category.
2. Take the A priorities and decide which is the most important item — the one task that must be done that day. That becomes Al, the next most important is A2 and so forth.
3. Always work on the As before going to Cs.

NOTE: On occasion you need to step away from a major task. You'll want to get your eyes off the computer screen or yourself out of a chair. After you take a break, you may want to come back and tackle one small task that is lower on the priority list. If it's something you can do quickly and efficiently, do it. By interspersing low-priority items you can dispense with quickly, you shorten your list. That's a feel-good achievement and may leave you better prepared to return to the major task. This approach isn't for everyone, but it may work for you.

How to Cope with Hectic Days

- *You need all the help you can get to keep up with time management tasks when things are frenzied.*
- *Don't fight fate.*
- *Know your job inside and out.*
- *Be prepared. Anticipate potential problems and solutions.*
- *Don't promise more than you can realistically handle.*
- *Take a break; get a beverage or take a short walk.*
- *Work efficiently. Don't procrastinate.*
- *Keep your wits about you. Do not get distracted.*
- *Make sure you have all relevant information before making a decision.*
- *Keep an attitude that says, "I will get this done."*
- *Stay lighthearted. Learn to laugh at yourself and at situations that could otherwise be stressful.*
- *Focus on answers, not problems.*

How to Deal with Revolving Bosses

Whether it's the nature of your industry or an unstable economy, many workers can find themselves adrift because of frequent changes in the management ranks. But a revolving door of bosses doesn't mean you can't thrive despite the instability. Here are some tips to keep your career on track:

- *Get to know your latest boss's style and priorities ASAP. Like working with any boss, it's always best to know what is expected of you. So when bosses come in, ask about the results they expect within the immediate future (six months), how often they like to be kept apprised of progress and how much they want to be involved in specific problems.*
- *Roll up your sleeves. Don't unload your gripes on new supervisors. Instead, let them know you're able and willing to tackle their biggest challenges.*

- *Develop strong relationships with coworkers. Working with a stable group of peers can help you stay focused on serving internal customers.*
- *Maintain a positive attitude. Difficult as it may be to stay upbeat in a situation where your bosses may not even stick around long enough to know your last name, it's imperative that you give each new supervisor a fair shake.*
- *Build relationships with upper management. Keep higher-level managers in the know on your accomplishments. So regarding yourself with each new supervisor, there are people higher up who know your capabilities well. Consider asking a senior manager to be your mentor.*

Be More Productive Without Working Longer Hours (Yes, You Can!)

For many, the five-day, 40-hour workweek is a distant memory. More individuals than ever before are putting in 10 or more hours a day at the office. In fact, in a recent survey of 141 workers conducted by Steelcase, more than half of those polled said that despite frequent changes in bosses, they work more than 40 hours a week. A third said they take work home at least one night a week. One way to avoid longer hours in the office is to prioritize your time and redefine your workplace parameters. Here are some ways to make your workdays shorter and more productive:

- *Call at choice times of the day. Initiate phone calls just before lunch or near the close of the day, when the other party is more likely to keep the conversation brief.*
- *Handle a piece of paper only once and act on it immediately. Don't move it from one pile to another.*
- *Follow an agenda. When a telephone conversation or meeting digresses, bring it back around, promising to discuss the other issues later.*

- *Get organized. Maintain clearly marked files so you can stop wasting precious time searching for misplaced documents.*
- *Recognize your peak energy times. Do the tough tasks when your energy level is at its highest. Save routine work for low points of the day.*

Be Alert About Wasting Time

We complain that we never have enough time, but a lot of the reason is because we waste it. Consider the following:

- **You begin your day without a plan of action.**
  If you have no plan for how you'll tackle your workload, you'll end up enslaved to other demands. Manage your time by doing the right things, not by doing things quicker.

- **You keep a messy workspace.**
  A minute spent here, a minute spent there looking for stuff is a huge time waster. A person with a messy desk uses one and a half hours a day looking for things or being easily distracted.

- **You cheat yourself from sleep.**
  Lack of sleep increases your stress level and intensifies feelings of lack of control. You'll spend time at work aimlessly, wishing you weren't so tired.

- **You don't take a break.**
  You're wasting time if you don't get out of the building for lunch. Taking lunch time outside the office or a brief breather from the day recharges the batteries and keeps us more productive.

Time

Time management has always been a challenge for business professionals, and it will continue to be a challenge. People thought technology would make their lives simpler and reduce paper pile-up in the office. That really hasn't happened. Some employees complain of having more paper because now they print out e-mail messages in addition to their regular mail.

There are probably many days you feel like there just aren't enough hours to get done what you need to do. We can't stop time from passing, and we can't stop the clock or turn the hands back an hour or two. However, we can manage our thoughts and projects, and establish priorities. We all have the same number of hours in a day. What we do with them and how we manage our tasks is up to us.

Remember: Time is precious. Once it has passed, it is gone forever.

Be Aware of These Time Wasters

- *Inability to say no*

  Of course you want to be helpful, but what if you are already swamped? How do you decide when to say no to a request? Ask yourself if this is a part or extension of your job. If not, is it a way to advance your career, or are you being taken advantage of. Do you feel right about it? If it's your supervisor making the request, you need to discuss your concerns with him or her. Expect the unexpected to occur during the day.

- *Crises*

  A crisis is an unexpected interruption of major impact, above and beyond the normal day's events, that requires your immediate attention. Expect the unexpected to occur during your day. Head off crises by finding out why things keep going wrong and learning to anticipate the outcome of events. When a crisis does occur, minimize its impact by being proactive in thinking your actions through rather than just reacting. Flexibility is critical to being a successful time manager.

- *Managing events*

  Establish some quiet time throughout the day to get yourself reorganized and mentally back on track. Ask yourself: "What am I thinking about right now?" If it's not about the task you're supposed to be doing, you won't be as effective.

Do not squander time, for that's the stuff life is made of.

— Ben Franklin

How Quickly Time Flies

There are many things throughout the day that can waste our time. They may not seem significant by themselves, but add them up and they can equal minutes or even hours of wasted time!

How Quickly Time Flies	
Get morning beverage, say hello to coworkers, unpack desk	20 min.
Stop in hall throughout the day to speak with coworkers	45 min.
Take time in restroom to visit with coworker	20 min.
Extended lunch and breaks	30 min.
Personal telephone calls	<u>20 min.</u>
	135 min.
	or
	2.25 hrs!

Time Robbers

Factors Externally Imposed	Factors Self-generated
Telephone interruptions	Lack of good organization
Meetings	Unrealistic time estimation/job
Social visiting	Trying to do too much
Other people's deadlines	Lack of delegation
Unexpected delays	Snap decisions that backfire
Mistakes of others	Failure to listen
Paperwork and reports	Lack of motivation
Poor communication	Inability to say no
Outside activities	Making all decisions yourself
Employees with problems	No system of self-accountability
Responding to crises	Not keeping daily project list
Customer complaints	Confused responsibilities
Too much routine work	Lack of creative effort
Unexpected interruptions	Procrastination

Activity: Consider your own *time robbers*. List factors under each category that rob you of most of your time.

Factors Externally Imposed	Factors Self-generated

The Time Management Spectrum

We don't really manage time. Time is going to pass whether we want it to or not. Instead, we manage ourselves, our thoughts and our work. We manage the completion of tasks, the scheduling of meetings and the handling of interruptions. You can't control time, but you can control how you spend it.

- *Do it now!*
- *Keep an up-to-date job manual.*
- *Focus on tasks of high value.*

- *Plan every day.*
- *Clarify objectives.*
- *Anticipate crises.*
- *Delegate; knowing how, when and to whom to delegate is the first step toward successful time management.*
- *Control telephone interruptions.*
- *Select and implement a planning system that will work for you.*
- *Keep lists.*
- *Set realistic goals.*
- *Set deadline dates — an absolute must!*
- *Search for alternatives — a simpler, faster way.*
- *To cope with overload, take a break.*
- *Think about a new or different approach.*
- *Think about something else for awhile.*
- *Write a to-do List and assign priorities.*
- *Clean up your office.*
- *Examine your current work habits and make adjustments for greater efficiency.*
- *Have a positive attitude about your work and your ability to control it.*
- *Know what you need to accomplish during the work day.*
- *Recognize what time of day you are most productive.*
- *Always write things down. Don't rely on your memory; you have too much to remember.*
- *Always confirm your appointments.*
- *Record how your time is being used.*
- *Concentrate on goals.*
- *Do the right things right the first time.*
- *Relax when you ought to be relaxing.*
- *Put up notes and signs as constant reminders of your goals.*
- *When involved in discussions, stick to the issue at hand.*
- *Don't waste your time and energy on non-productive activities or conversations.*

- *Learn to think on paper.*
- *Finish what you start; don't jump around.*
- *Take time to prepare for tomorrow.*
- *Spend five minutes in the morning and afternoon mentally prioritizing.*
- *Excuse yourself from idle chatter after a few minutes.*
- *Don't confuse...*
  - Activity with RESULTS.
  - Hard work with RESULTS.
  - Efficiency with RESULTS.

Efficiency is doing things right. Effectiveness is doing the right things. But you can waste time being efficient at the wrong task or doing the right tasks poorly.

Then & Now — A Looking-Glass View

Then: The office looked different. The support person accepted the status quo and didn't try to streamline activities.

Now: More time-tracking software is available, along with other modern-day tools. Time, however, isn't made more or less productive; you are. The *inner circle* professional stays focused and differentiates between what brings the company value versus what is essentially busywork. He or she is quick to say, "It's crazy around here, and there's got to be a better way to do things. I've got to figure it out!"

BECOME AN INNER CIRCLE ASSISTANT

How to be a Star in Your Profession and Achieve *Inner Circle* Status

I READ JOAN'S BOOK

Today is _____, and I, _____,
finished reading the book *Become an Inner Circle Assistant* by Joan
M. Burge.

I have been thoroughly exposed to this valuable information
and shall use it to become a member of (or to maintain my position in) that exclusive group of employees. This certificate is intended to help me alert management, colleagues and other
interested parties that I settle for nothing less than excellence in
almost everything I do. Joan's book reminds me that often excellence is attainable as the result of combined effort. When this certificate is placed in my employee file or displayed, it is intended to
serve as a declaration of this commitment to myself, my employer
and all those with whom I interact each and every business day.

**To receive your official certificate, complete the information
below and mail to: Office Dynamics, Ltd., 2766 Evening Rock
St., Las Vegas, NV 89135**

Please Print:

Name: _____

Company Name: _____

Address: _____

_____

City: _____ State: _____ Zip: _____

BECOME A WORLD CLASS
ADMINISTRATIVE ASSISTANT™
A HIGH-LEVEL BOOT CAMP
PRESENTED BY JOAN BURGE

Discount Coupon

You're invited to attend one session at a reduced price. You've demonstrated your interest in becoming an *inner circle* administrative professional by reading or showing an interest in my book *Become an Inner Circle Assistant*. And it will be my pleasure to greet you in the workshop setting.

This discount coupon entitles you to a savings of five percent off the current advertised price for the *Become a World Class Administrative Assistant™* High-Level Boot Camp, held in Las Vegas, Nevada.

For workshop details, agenda and registration information, visit www.officedynamicsltd.com/becoming_a_wcaa.html. This certificate may not be used in combination with other offers and has no cash value.

This certificate expires June 1, 2006.

OFFICE DYNAMICS, LTD.
2766 Evening Rock Street, Las Vegas, NV 89135
800-STAR-139
www.officedynamicsltd.com
E-mail: jburge@officedynamicsltd.com

GOOD NEWS! Discount has been extended indefinitely! Call 800-STAR-139 to register for the workshop and apply your discount today!

INDEX

ABOUT THE AUTHOR

Joan Burge is North America's foremost administrative expert, trainer, consultant and motivational speaker. She is the founder and CEO of Office Dynamics, Ltd., an international leader in the development and presentation of sophisticated training programs and information for administrative office professionals. Joan has more than 30 years of experience in the administrative profession as well as in the fields of training, speaking entrepreneurship and innovation. As a professional speaker, corporate trainer, consultant and author, Joan equips administrative professionals to move beyond task work to higher-level functions, to meet the ever-changing demands of today's workplace. Joan works with high-level executives to ensure they are fully utilizing the talents of their assistants and provides insight into how they can improve their overall working relationships.

Joan is best known for her Star Achievement Series®, a tri-level, 12-part curriculum designed to bring out the star performance in administrative assistants and support staff. She is the creator and host of the *Annual Forum for Administrative Professionals*, held each fall in various parts of the country; creator of a three-day, high-level boot camp for assistants, called *Become a World Class Assistant*™, which is held in Las Vegas; and creator of the *How to Maximize the Time & Talents of Your Assistant*™ seminar for executives. Joan has provided guidance, continuity of purpose and mentoring to administrative professionals and their managers. Her programs have resulted in significant productivity increases to her clients, including Caterpillar Inc., Humana Inc., The Boeing Co., The Schwan Food Company, Churchill Downs, Nokia,

US Airways, Intel, Rockwell Collins, The Marriott Corporation and The Children's Hospital of Philadelphia.

Joan is the author of three books and 12 workbooks, is the editor of *Monday Motivators*™ and has been published in more than 54 trade journals. She is also featured with television star Jennifer O'Neill in a book called *Remarkable Women* and is a contributing author of *Real World Communication Strategies That Work*. Joan is a member of the American Society for Training & Development, the National Speakers Association, the Southern Nevada Human Resource Association, the National Association of Female Executives and the Las Vegas Chamber of Commerce.

Prior to launching Office Dynamics, Ltd., Joan worked as an administrative professional in 12 different companies, in five states, over a 20-year period. During that time, she applied her skills in both small offices and magnificent Fortune 500 companies. Having worked in some of the best and worst environments to be found anywhere, she not only thrived in the field but learned how to become an *inner circle* assistant to a several different company CEOs.

Contact Joan at:
Office Dynamics, Ltd.
2766 Evening Rock Street
Las Vegas, NV 89135
800-STAR-139 ◆ www.officedynamicsltd.com ◆
jburge@officedynamicsltd.com

NOTES